The Gilded Age Revisited

An Ironic Reflection from Opulence

Aaron Locklear, MSc.HRM, MBA

© **Copyright 2024 by** – Aaron Locklear. **All rights reserved.**

The transmission, duplication, or reproduction of any of the following work, including specific information, will be considered illegal, whether done electronically or in print. This extends to creating a secondary, or tertiary copy of the work or a recorded document and is only allowed with express written consent from the publisher. All additional rights reserved.

Table of Contents

Preface 5

Part I: The Original Gilded Age – A Tale of Progress and Plutocracy 8

1: Seeds of Splendor – The Post-Civil War Boom 9

2: Magnates and Moguls – Titans of Industry 13

3: The Silver Lining – Innovations and Inventions 17

4: Labor Takes a Stand – Unrest in the Industrial Jungle 21

5: High Society – The Glimpse of Elegance 25

6: The Politician's Ballet – Dancing with Corruption 28

7: Shadows of the Metropolis – Urban Growth and Decay 32

8: The Farmers' Rebellion – Populism's Early Cry 35

9: The Haymarket Affair – A Prelude to Rights 38

10: The Panic of 1893 – A Golden Collapse 42

11: Literature of the Gilded Age – The Pen's Irony 45

12: The Long Goodbye – Transitioning to the Progressive Era 49

Part II: Echoes of the Gilded Age in 2025 – A Familiar Melody 53

13: The Second Coming – Economic Reverberations 54

14: Modern-Day Moguls – The Tech Titans 58

15: Innovation for the Few – Tech's Golden Curtain 61

16: Labor's New Voice – A Gig Economy Reality 65

17: The Socialite Revival – Redefining Opulence 68

18: Political Theatre Redux – Lobbyists and their Legislators 72

19: Metropolis Redux – Tech Hubs and the Urban Divide 76

20: Rural Voices Rise – Echoes of Farmer Populism 80

21: Protest and Pushback – Modern-Day Labor Movements 84

22: Financial Deja Vu – The Boom-Bust Cycle Returns 88

23: Literary Reflections – A New Age of Satire 92

24: Intermission Interrupted – The Case for Reformation 96

25: The Invisible Line – Bridging Past and Present 100

26: A Gilded Future 104

Epilogue 107

Appendix 110

Endnote 115

Preface

In a world that perpetually spins toward the extraordinary, seldom do the echoes of history resound with quite the clarity as they do when we stumble—ironically, almost delightfully—into the same pitfalls our predecessors once did. "The Gilded Age Revisited: An Ironic Reflection from Opulence" ushers its readers into a mirrored hall where the late 19th century elegantly waltzes with the early 21st century, a dance as graceful as it is ill-advised. For those who consider history a discipline of memorization, the tale of the Gilded Age offers a saucy reminder that revisiting the excesses of yore right here, in 2025, reads less like a cautionary tale and more like a favored rerun.

The Gilded Age, gilded rather than golden—perhaps a nod to Mark Twain's witty derision—invites us to explore an era bloated with wealth, yet riddled with disparity. It was a time when industrial magnates, dubbed with reverent cynicism as "Robber Barons," constructed empires atop the twin pillars of relentless ambition and breathtaking inequity. The parallels in social tapestry, between then and now, flutter like the delicate wings of a historical butterfly, disquieting in their striking similarity. Our intention is not to scold but to entertain with a nod and a wink; for who among us hasn't guiltily reveled in luxury interspersed with the ignoble, much like the society of 2025 finds itself doing?

As we traverse through this ironic exposition, it is crucial to embrace the narrative with both a wry smile and a discerning gaze. The corridors of power and the economic chasm have found new architects in billionaires wielding technology instead of railroads, while the teeming underclass—the engine of industry—now powers the digital universe, often with correspondingly meager returns. Our tale here serves to entertain yet enlighten, and while irony seasons our script, it remains rooted in earnest inquiry.

Innovation, the charming mantra of both the Railway Age and the Information Age, carries with it the dual-edged sword of transformation and turbulence. Then, it reshaped the city skyline, and now, it penetrates the very essence of global human interaction. The transcontinental railroad's relentless march finds its digital redux in streams of data coursing through fiber optics, fueling economies no less voracious in their demands. Our examination reveals how the knitted fabric of social structure is challenged anew, spun into patterns painstakingly familiar, if not utterly ironic.

Thus, dear reader, as we embark on this journey into the past and its resurrection in our present, it is our modest endeavor to unveil the elegant—if somewhat sardonic—dance of prosperity and poverty, of progress and paralysis. "The Gilded Age Revisited" encourages you to ponder how a nation, in its majestic glide through time, manages both to emulate and exceed its former opulence.

So, are we hopelessly ensnared in the cycles of history, gyrating in an enduring masquerade of wealth and want, or are we conversing with our better angels through the guise of gilded irony? As the rebuttals to such inquiries ruminate upon the page, may you discern in them the hidden harmonies, the playful dissonance, and perhaps—just perhaps—a blueprint for a future that wields its gilded lessons wisely.

PART I

The Original Gilded Age – A Tale of Progress and Plutocracy

Chapter 1: Seeds of Splendor – The Post-Civil War Boom

As the dust settled on the battlefields of the American Civil War, a metamorphosis began, transforming a war-torn nation into a burgeoning powerhouse. In the immediate aftermath, what rose from the ashes was neither a phoenix of equality nor unity but rather a creature of one-sided splendor. The economic boom of the post-Civil War era was a gilded affair, draped in irony and disparity, marked by the opulence of the few and the backbreaking labor of the many.

In this freshly minted nation, where the ink on the Thirteenth Amendment had barely dried, the grand promise of freedom quickly morphed into a new reality—one where "freedom" was often more synonymous with opportunity for capital gain than with social liberty or equality. Railroads sliced through the heartland like steel arteries, carrying with them not just passengers and freight but the concentrated wealth of industrial magnates whose names, like Carnegie, Rockefeller, and Vanderbilt would echo through the corridors of American history.

The crux of this economic ascent lay in the advantageous shift from agrarian roots to industrial prowess. The war had created a formidable impetus for technological advancement and infrastructure growth. Factories sprung up like mushrooms after the rain, their smokestacks reaching ambitiously towards the heavens, heralding a new age. At the same time, the vast troves of coal, iron, and oil nestled beneath American soil provided the bedrock for burgeoning industries. As if preordained by destiny, this raw potential found itself harnessed—and inevitably hoarded—by a select cadre of entrepreneurs whose genius for business was matched only by their appetite for accumulation.

They hailed this period as the dawning of a golden era, yet the shine bore a striking resemblance to the superficial gleam of gold-plated lead. The wealth generated by this industrial boom precariously balanced on the shoulders of the labor force—the unsung heroes, whose sweat and toil were often compensated with meager wages and grueling working conditions. Immigrants, fresh off ships and infused with dreams of prosperity, found themselves enmeshed in the tangled webs of tenement housing and twelve-hour shifts, their promised land turning rapidly into a landscape of deferred dreams.

This concentration of wealth did not occur in the shadows but rather unfolded in a blinding, public spectacle. Lavish mansions lined the streets of New York and Boston, and socialites draped in the latest

Parisian fashions became fodder for burgeoning media outlets. Ironically, this era, so hailed for its prosperity, left glaring gaps of disparity that foreshadowed future unrest. The Gilded Age, as Mark Twain so aptly dubbed it, sparkled not with the brilliance of universal prosperity, but rather with the fractured light of a chandelier—beautiful from afar, precariously hung, and ultimately illuminating only the chosen few who danced beneath it.

In policy spheres, politicians were seduced by the intoxicating allure of laissez-faire economics, draping the halls of government with policies that ensured minimal interference with these industrial titans. With regulatory shadows barely cast, it should come as no surprise that wealth accumulation by individuals like the Rockefellers and Vanderbilts skyrocketed, paralleling the grandiosity of their social and economic influence.

While the captains of industry feasted upon lavish banquets, the labor class held their children, straight-backed and somber-eyed, beneath dining tables whose stolen crumbs might bring brief solace. These early murmurs of economic inequality, so easily swept under the ostentatious carpets of gilded ballrooms, were seeds of discord being sown beneath the very foundations of industrial progress.

The irony of this chapter in American history reveals itself not just in the glittering surfaces but in the shadows they cast—a story of progress intertwined with exploitation, brilliance overshadowed by inequity. As we unravel the layers of this Gilded Age, we are reminded that while roads of gold may lead the way for a nation, it is often the gravel beneath them that tells the true story of its journey.

Chapter 2: Magnates and Moguls – Titans of Industry

In the grand tapestry of America's economic history, few figures shine more luminescent than the titans of the Gilded Age—John D. Rockefeller, Andrew Carnegie, and Cornelius Vanderbilt. These magnates, with their unquenchable thirst for progress and profit, sculpted the modern industrial landscape with a finesse and fervor previously unseen. They were the visionaries who saw an unrefined wilderness and left behind a sprawling metropolis; the alchemists who transformed the black gold of Oil Creek and the cold veins of Pennsylvania's iron mines into the lifeblood of the nation. As we peel back the layers of their gilded exploits, we find not only empires built on oil, steel, and rail, but also an ironic reflection on the true cost of their ambitions—a monopoly on not just industry, but innovation itself.

To remark only on their unimaginable success is to write a chapter without acknowledging its shadow— the spirit of competition, sacrificed at the altar of monopolistic ambition. The irony lies in how these paragons of capitalism, in their singular quest to consolidate, accumulate, and control, inadvertently throttled the dynamism that competition is supposed to engender. With a deft sleight of hand unseen since the days of Jedediah Strutt, Rockefeller secured his

Standard Oil's dominance not by the obliteration of his rivals, but through the more civil, some might say Byzantine, art of acquisition and integration.

John D. Rockefeller, the patriarch of petroleum, embraced an ethos the ancients would recognize: order must come from chaos. As the cacophony of oil rigs crescendoed across America, Rockefeller quietly maneuvered among his competitors like a maestro wielding a baton. He orchestrated success through horizontal integration—a polite term for subsuming one's rivals to craft a single, unassailable archivist of control. Under his stewardship, the bits and pieces of fragmented oil interests were woven together into a grand tapestry bound by the trust of Standard Oil. The consumer and competitor alike were left largely spectators to Rockefeller's opus, applauding innovation while lamenting the diminished stage of free enterprise.

Andrew Carnegie, in the steel-forging furnaces, pursued a similarly paradoxical strategy. With his fabled rags-to-riches story, Carnegie came to epitomize the American Dream—now available exclusively through the purchase of a consolidated single-ticket transaction. Carnegie's drive to control the entire steel production line, from raw iron ore to finished rail, was the embodiment of vertical integration. With each acquisition, the once wild and untamed spirit of market variability was neatly brought to heel. Ironically, this titan who funded libraries and championed education—both beacons of free thought—stood as the architect of an industry structure that educated competitors in futility rather than innovation.

And let's not forget Cornelius Vanderbilt, the Commodore. From steamboats to railroads, Vanderbilt's enterprises carved channels through the nation's growth, much like his business practices carved potential competition out of existence. His commodious control of rail lines could almost have been mistaken for a public service—were it not conducted for such extraordinary private gain. With each railroad spike driven, the competition's course was rerouted to accommodate VPR—Vanderbilt's Personal Railways.

The enduring irony is that these titans, whose very livelihoods depended on the exceptionalism of the American marketplace, were the very figures who circumscribed its competitive spirit. In their insatiable quest for profit and efficiency, they hatched an industrial autarky that left many by the wayside. The same era that witnessed skyscrapers scratching the heavens also watched as the entrepreneurial ladder was enveloped in clouds of monopolistic haze.

It is tempting to romanticize the grandiloquent legacy left by Rockefeller, Carnegie, and Vanderbilt. Yet, as we stand on the forward edge of the industry's horizon in 2025, one cannot help but glance backward in curiosity at what could have been had competition not been systematically enfeebled. What transformative technologies and entrepreneurial spirits were silenced, cocooned, or dissuaded in this age of empire without borders? Alas, the Gilded Age's titans, though hailed luminaries of heliotropic ambition, left behind a paradox: a visionary's landscape supersaturated with cement but eerily barren of the nimble saplings that competition fosters.

As we revisit this age from our modern vantage point, we celebrate their indomitable spirits and pirouetting shades of progress, all the while mourning the competition they so elegantly eclipsed. Who can say unequivocally whether the price was worth the gold-plated ticket to progress? But then again, such questions cost far less when they don't need to be asked over the roar of dynamism echoing through a truly free market.

Chapter 3: The Silver Lining – Innovations and Inventions

The Gilded Age, that illustrious epoch where fortunes were amassed with the solemnity of a prayer service interrupted by enthusiastic coin counting, was indeed a period rich with technological advances. Perhaps it was the twinkling allure of golden light reflecting off pocket watches and cane handles that inspired a generation to transform society through innovation. One could argue, with a sense of irony best savored slowly, that the real triumphs of this era were the breakthroughs in technology and infrastructure that laid the foundation for the modern world.

In the reverent halls of innovation, electricity can be considered the exalted priest delivering salvation to a world previously shrouded in shadow. Thomas Edison, that benevolent sage of Menlo Park, graced society with the incandescent light bulb in 1879. A marvel it was, rendering obsolete the flickering gas lamps that had danced so romantically on cobblestone streets. Edison's pursuit of illuminating not just homes but also the prospects of progress stood like a lighthouse guiding humanity through darkness. Yet, some might argue (with just a smidgen of sarcasm) that his greater contribution was in giving financiers a new toy to invest in, and occasionally understand.

If electricity was the priest, then steel was the bedrock altar on which modernity was built. Andrew Carnegie, a name synonymous with unrestrained entrepreneurship and perhaps excessive feathering of one's nest, revolutionized steel production with the Bessemer process. This cheaper and more efficient method of producing steel was the backbone for skyscrapers that would soon kiss the heavens and for the railroads that wove the American landscape together like a rich tapestry of opportunity. Cities swelled literally and figuratively with tall tales of ambition. Yet, amidst these iron giants and ironclad contracts, there lay the shimmering silver lining of societal progress.

Indeed, the unfortunate overshadowing of these substantial feats by the proverbial glint of gold coinage cannot be overstated. Where there were tracks of commerce being laid, there were also tracks of dubious deals being hatched, with fortunes flipping like well-oiled coins. Transcontinental railroads were not just symbols of connectivity but also theaters of high drama, where fortunes were both forged and frittered away under the gilded tutelage of what we might generously call "creative accounting."

Alas, innovations of this gilded period were not confined to the electrical or the metallic. Alexander Graham Bell, perhaps driven by the cacophony of endless telegraph clicks, presented us with the telephone in 1876—a device that not only revolutionized communication but also ensured that social niceties could be politely sidestepped with the phrase "The caller you have reached is not available." Yet, Bell's invention was more than an avoidance tool. It was evidence of the era's determination to string together the far-flung corners of America with spoken word, albeit transmitted with the same cackling inefficiencies that perennially plague new technology.

The typewriter, introduced by Christopher Latham Sholes, complemented the telephone by transforming the tedious art of handwritten correspondence into a brisk, surprisingly mechanical affair. Businesses embraced it as both an essential tool and, presumably, a means of wielding an impressive array of indented papers and copious carbon copies. In offices across the land, clerks were being introduced to the symphonic clatter of typebars, heralding a new age where efficiency met standardization—albeit at the cost of many ink-stained cuffs and crumb-drenched desk drawers.

Indeed, the Gilded Age, with its unapologetic zeal for newness, seemed to suggest that human genius was not only embodied in the shimmering tantalum of gold but in the spark of an electric filament, the tensile strength of a steel rail, and the telephone's nascent promise of connected corridors of conversation. However, it is essential to acknowledge—appreciatively, with a chortle—that the gold rush, whether literal or metaphorical, often seeks to gild not just the lily but nearly everything that sprouted alongside progress.

Perhaps, as an ironic nod to this era's ingenuity and greed, future historians will reflect: Was it the marvels of innovation that truly drove the Gilded Age, or was it merely those gold-tipped dreams that endowed it with its lasting, if ironic, sheen? In the pursuit of understanding this paradox, one must simultaneously embrace the ambition of invention and the gleam of illusive gain; for it is within this silken mesh of earnest endeavor and entangled aspirations that the true legacy of the Gilded Age resides.

Chapter 4: Labor Takes a Stand – Unrest in the Industrial Jungle

As the smoke of progress billowed from the factory chimneys of the Gilded Age, an irony of monumental proportions took root beneath its sooty disguise. The era was characterized by its sparkling veneers, a facade of prosperity that seemingly never dulled. Yet, hidden beneath this iridescent glow, the very souls who powered this machine were engulfed in darkness. The hands that toiled long hours under grueling conditions received no glimmer of the prosperity they forged. Indeed, it was the laborers of this time—the spirited yet weary cogs within the great industrial contraption—who mounted an extraordinary stand against an empire that so effortlessly brushed them aside.

The late 19th century in America was a playground for the titans of industry whose wealth could rival the opulence of European monarchies. Behind every railroad spike hammered into the continental expanse, every spool of cotton spun into elegant garments, and every steel beam erected toward the sky, were workers subjected to a reality bereft of safety nets. They drudged through ten, twelve, and even fourteen-hour shifts, often in the most perilous of conditions, their efforts lining the pockets of magnates with silver. How ironic, we might muse, that while fortunes erupted like geysers for the fortunate few, the laborers were left tending to barren fields of prosperity.

Turning to the bustling avenues of New York, Chicago, and Pittsburgh, one witnessed the crescendo of discontent taking shape. Laborers, diminished in both voice and recompense, united in a collective effort to reclaim their dignity. Their awakening was not a gentle one; it was forged in fires of desperation but tempered with the resolve of hope. Sarah Bagley in the textile mills, George Pullman's railcar constructors, and the steel workers in Andrew Carnegie's formidable mills gathered under the banner of unity. They demanded what seemed the simplest of human dignities—fair wages, reasonable working hours, and safe environments. The very notion of having to bargain for these non-negotiables speaks to an epoch marinated in paradox.

The rise of labor movements like the Knights of Labor and the American Federation of Labor in the 1880s and 1890s marked a turning point that would redefine the economic landscape of the United States. Strikes became the resounding voice of the unheard. The Haymarket Affair of 1886, though initially a campaign for an eight-hour workday, manifested as a tragic deflowering of peaceful protest into chaos—yet it did awaken a national dialogue on the conditions of American workers. Herein lies the ultimate irony: the more fervently these industrialists attempted to suppress the labor movement, the more vibrant and resolute it became.

Consider also the Pullman Strike of 1894, a plea ignited by cuts in wages without corresponding reductions in rent for company-owned housing—a pinch felt even through the extravagant silk lining of industrial wealth. This nationwide action paralyzed the railways, with workers staunchly incurring the wrath of federal intervention. They were branded as radicals and anarchists—a cruel jest, considering they sought merely to carve out a place within the American Dream that had so eagerly accepted their contributions.

As we stroll through the avenues of history to the contemporary metropolis of 2025, the irony persists. What began as a struggle for humane conditions has evolved into a nuanced battle over automation, gig economies, and a living wage fit for an era of digital omnipresence. The labor force, once muscle-bound and soot-covered, now often find their grievances translated into codes and algorithms.

Peering through the lens of time, it is rather befitting to conclude that the labor movements of the Gilded Age did not merely tilt at windmills of inequity; they planted the seeds of future revolutions within the global labor market. They schooled generations to come that progress, however gilded, begins and must end with those who propel it forward. Let us appreciate, then, the tenacity of those laborers who dared to disrupt their industrial confines. For in their struggle lies a testament to the inconsistency of an age that promised enlightenment yet delivered encumbrance—an irony not lost through the annals of history.

Chapter 5: High Society – The Glimpse of Elegance

In the dazzling theater of the Gilded Age, the curtain rose nightly on scenes of opulence and grandeur, casting a gilded spotlight upon the elite, whose very existence seemed a defiant rebuke to the more mundane laws of gravity and necessity. As if choreographed on a celestial stage, the upper echelons of society waltzed through an era defined not by the steel and sweat that erected the towering cities, but by the golden veneers that shimmered over grand ballrooms.

These palatial gatherings were more than mere social events; they were declarations of status, manifestos of wealth unfurled in the form of diamond-studded tiaras, velvet gowns, and pearls that appeared like teardrops of the moon strung upon delicate threads. Indeed, who needs the common affections of societal fraternité when one can exchange a knowing glance over a cascade of champagne, beside hand-painted porcelain vases that likely cost more than the average worker's lifetime earnings?

Balls were often hosted in the extravagant mansions lining Fifth Avenue, and in the palacial spaces of

Newport, names that dripped with old money and whispered ambitions: Vanderbilt, Astor, and Carnegie. These families orchestrated their soirées like symphonies, ensuring each crescendo coincided with the opulence of their meticulously adorned homes—abodes so grand they seemed to mock the very concept of shelter, presenting instead a feast for the eyes, each detail yearning to draw a gasp of astonishment: crystal chandeliers dangling like stars captured mid-fall, mirrors that stretched endlessly to replicate not just space but the illusion of eternity itself.

Yet, ironically, as these elite circles danced their pirouettes across marble floors, the reality beyond their silken curtains was anything but elegant. A glance out the frosted windows, had they cared for more than their own reflections, might have revealed the slums, the tenements, and the sweatshops where the less fortunate toiled, their existence barely registering as a footnote in the glittering biographies of the season's social darlings.

In truth, the juxtaposition of high society and urban poverty painted a picture only an era so grandiosely royal in its sins could produce. The air inside was perfumed, perhaps to veil the scent of want that wafted in from the alleys outside. Roads, ostensibly paved with the metaphorical gold extracted by industrial barons, were indeed cobbled with the desperate hands of child laborers and immigrants.

Meanwhile, discussions within these opulent halls often lavished attention on such noble topics as art, literature, and philanthropy—a civic duty that often saw pennies worth of generosity trickling down, while dollars continued to fertilize the roots of their growing genealogical trees. Those outside could yearn for no more than wisps of the roast beef's aroma that occasionally drifted from the opulent kitchens, where haute cuisine found itself wasted upon those who dined more to be seen than to eat.

In this era, irony wove itself through the fabric of society like the gold thread in a debutante's first gown. Here, to be blind was not merely a choice but a fashion, a lifestyle; to build walls of wealth so high that even sound struggled to traverse, ensuring laughter within would never mingle with cries without.

Thus, the Gilded Age waltzed forward, a curiously choreographed duet between elegance and ignorance, reminding future generations—those in the famed hindsight of 2025—that the grandeur of the privileged can sometimes obscure the very humanity it pretends to celebrate. A gilded age, indeed, where beneath the shimmer lay a landscape steeped in the shadows of societal neglect—a lesson, it seems, that the opulence of a few often comes at the silent expense of the many.

Chapter 6: The Politician's Ballet – Dancing with Corruption

In the grand theater of American history, few performances have been as enduring and enigmatic as the intricate ballet between politicians and the industrial titans of the Gilded Age. This spectacle, masterfully choreographed over decades, unfolded not merely on the stages of power in Washington but reverberated through the corridors of burgeoning corporations. This dance, as it ebbed and flowed, was as much a work of art as it was a reflection of the era's burgeoning opulence and its ironic contradictions.

In the dusty corridors of Congress, where bills were introduced with grandiosity, legislative processes took on the guise of an elaborate waltz. Politicians donned their finest rhetorical garb, moving effortlessly in tandem with the silent orchestration of industrial moguls who pulled the strings behind the scenes. These titans – the Carnegies, Vanderbilts, and Rockefellers of their time – were the maestros of this unprecedented performance, conducting their symphony of success using the well-rehearsed notes of influence and, admittedly, corruption.

The politicians, with their choreographed nods and knowing winks, were not just willing participants but dedicated students of this grand ballet. Each move was deliberate; each pause emphasized the unsaid agreements forged in private retreats and smoke-filled rooms. Legislative decisions that supposedly served the public interest often bore the distinct signature of corporate interests – a gentle reminder of who really penned the script.

In this dance, political leaders wove a delicate tapestry of policies that, on the surface, promised prosperity and progress for all. Yet, just beneath this gleaming veneer lay the tangled threads of vested interests and selective benefaction. Tax codes were crafted with the precision of a pirouette, offering balletic tax breaks for industrial titans, all under the noble guise of stimulating growth and innovation. Railroads, steel mills, and oil companies stood as monumental beneficiaries, their lobbies echoing with applause as regulations quietly bowed out of the dancefloor.

Indeed, to achieve this perfect harmony, the dancers—our dear politicians—had to accommodate one additional layer to their routine: a deft balancing act. On one hand, they had to sway public opinion, promising reforms and touting the virtue of democracy. On the other, a less-publicized yet distinct role required greeting industrialists with open arms—a metaphorical curtsy—ensuring their coffers remained generously filled in return for favorable legislation. It was a spectacle that captured the essence of not just political theater but a genuine masterclass in irony.

With time, these interactions evolved into a more sophisticated ballet. New pas de deux emerged, as seen in the numerous ways politicians facilitated industrial prosperity. Granting land to railroads? With the precision of a perfect leap. Crafting monetary policy that seemed to exclusively favor industrial giants at the expense of the common worker? A graceful twirl. Each move, each decision, was a carefully calibrated note in the compositions of progress.

Even as the curtain began to close on the original Gilded Age, its legacy left a resounding impact on the American political stage. The dance, though perhaps more guarded, continued well into the 20th and 21st centuries, adding contemporary nuances to the original masterpiece. Politicians and corporatists now exchanged their waltzes for algorithms, their whispers for cryptic emails, yet the essence of their choreography remained painfully familiar.

Reflecting on this dance as we approach 2025, it's fascinating—not to mention a bit sardonic—to note how little has changed. While the attire of today's performers might appear more polished and groomed to evoke an image of transparency, the steps of this enduring ballet remain unmistakably consistent. With each political campaign financed by invisible hands, each legislative debate tipped subtly in favor of monolithic interest groups, the dance of our modern age makes an ironic nod to its Gilded predecessor.

Ultimately, this chapter in the American story isn't just about corruption or the co-opting of democracy. It's about the ballet—an intricate, time-honored dance that extends beyond dollars and votes, blending showmanship with governance and leaving us wondering if perhaps it is the dance itself, rather than its narrative, that is the true genius of the ages.

Chapter 7: Shadows of the Metropolis – Urban Growth and Decay

Marvel, if you will, at the audacious architectural phenomena of our urban landscapes. The burgeoning cities of the Gilded Age, with their towering marvels of steel and glass, stand as testaments to human ingenuity and ambition. In this period of unrestrained opulence, the skyline became mankind's ambitious exclamation mark against the canvas of the heavens. The edifices proudly announced a new era; yet, beneath their glistening facades, all was not as it seemed.

For every architectural triumph that scratched the sky, a labored, weary undertow pulled at the city's foundations — both literally and metaphorically. The architectural feats were the ever-visible symbols of progress, casting shadows that brilliantly masked the stark realities of life in the dim recesses of sprawling urban jungles. Indeed, it was a time when the allure of modernity almost convincingly concealed the squalor that festered below.

This era, championed by the vibrant hustle and promise of the metropolis, could ironically be described as one of unfortunate oversight when it came to its inhabitants. The wide boulevards that accommodated horse-drawn carriages and, later, the burgeoning tele-autos of the prosperous, failed to connect to the narrow alleyways cramped with tenements. These slums, often missed in the vibrant narrations of urban planners, housed the workforce that fueled the city's grinding gears, tucked neatly away out of sight and mind.

The grand corridors leading to the palisades and theaters whispered tales of Gatsby-esque indulgence, yet the adjacent byways groaned under the weight of poverty. The colossal bridges that boldly spanned rivers to connect districts also served, unwittingly, as conduits over the widening chasms of class.

Let us not overlook the ironies of hygiene and progress. Waterworks systems were celebrated in public discourse as engineering masterpieces, even as less publicized failures ensured that clean water was a privilege reserved for the discerning few. Sanitation departments grappled heroically with ever-mounting refuse, a problem exacerbated by society's penchant for consuming new luxuries while discarding the old at an unprecedented pace. Details such as these, inconvenient to the narrative of unbridled progress, were often obscured by the overwhelming desire to revel in the metropolis's upward thrust.

The evolution of public transit painted a similar picture of ironic reflection. As networks connected sprawling suburbs to commercial hearts, lauded as democratizing forces of mobility, they simultaneously became symbols of division. These trains, heralds of modernity, ferried individuals from the peripheries to the bustling city centers, yet their destinations remained subtly influenced by unspoken rules of segregation and socioeconomic hierarchy. The hum of progress, one mused, sounded oddly reminiscent of exclusion.

Thus, through the imperious skyline of the Gilded Age, an ironic lesson emerges: the grandeur of the city overshadowed the silent implosion of its human aspects. As resplendent as these cities gleamed from afar, drawing dreamers and captains of industry alike, they often neglected the moral architecture needed to sustain equitable growth.

And so it was that the era's most breathtaking achievements inadvertently sculpted the mold for urbanity's most persistent problems, teaching future generations — through stark relief and contrast — the complex dance between outward brilliance and inner decay. In the end, the Gilded Age's cities commendably reached for the stars yet struggled to reconcile the shadowed paths of their journeys on the ground below.

Chapter 8: The Farmers' Rebellion – Populism's Early Cry

Ah, the Gilded Age: where the glittering facades of mansion-dotted landscapes masked the simmering discontent of those who toiled in the shadows. While industrialists reveled in their monolithic titan statues, a quaint rebellion was brewing in the least glamorous of settings—America's rural farmlands. In this chapter, we shine a reverential spotlight on the farmers' heartfelt, albeit ironic, attempt to usurp their gilded overlords—a saga less like a climactic battle and more akin to a polite request to be noticed.

In the late 19th century, America's heartland pumped an agrarian rhythm that metronomically synced with the tilling of soil and the growth of golden grain swaying in the breeze. But alas, such idyllic pastoral scenery served as little more than the picturesque backdrop to a tempest of growing discontent. As industrial juggernauts and financiers amassed obscene wealth, farmers found themselves bound by the invisible handcuffs of oppressive railroad monopolies, unjust credit practices, and price-gouging middlemen. It turned out that the invisible hand of the market was less the guiding force of prosperity and more a greedy claw snatching away the fruits of their labor.

This mounting frustration soon gave life to what history would fondly (and ironically) commemorate as the Populist Movement—an early cry for fairness rendered in the rustic tongue of the countryside. The Farmers' Alliance, an assembly of rural underdogs, stitched together a patchwork quilt of grievances that would herald the rise of an authentic, albeit quaint, voice of outrage. They championed causes such as the regulation of railroads, the democratization of monetary policy through bimetallism, and the direct election of senators—ideas that bore the revolutionary zeal of toddlers rebelling against nap time.

Their torchbearer, and perhaps the most emblematic symbol of this discontent, emerged in the eloquence of William Jennings Bryan. With his biblical fervor captured in the famed "Cross of Gold" speech, Bryan rode the tidal wave of agrarian despair with a righteous indignation that was at once inspiring and tragically quixotic. Though he failed to ascend to the presidency, his oratory embalmed the era's populist sentiment in the annals of history—a poetic shout into the atmospheric silence above fields of neglected corn and wheat.

In urban drawing rooms, as cigar smoke hazed the visages of industrial magnates and their political puppets, the plight of these besieged cultivators may have seemed a comically distant concern. To the well-coiffed elite, these farmers were little more than obstinate relics from a bygone age, quaintly resisting the inevitable churn of progress. Yet, beneath their bucolic demeanor lay profound questions about equity, access, and representation—issues that would reverberate through the corridors of history with a persistence the originators could scarcely imagine.

Fast forward to 2025, and one might marvel at the familiarity of this narrative. The Gilded Age's farmers might find amusement in the modern contortions of rural and urban protesters wielding smartphones instead of pitchforks, yet the themes remain astonishingly consistent. The Déjà vu of economic exclusion persists, demonstrating the perennial nature of populism when inequality reaches a fever pitch.

Thus, as we close the chapter on Populism's early cry, we must appreciate the exquisite irony in how a movement once met with patronizing dismissal left unnoticed yet enduring imprints on the fabric of this nation's ethos. In their rebellion, these farmers taught us a beautiful hypocrisy: amid grand progress, the seeds of disenfranchisement are sown with breathtaking consistency. Although obscured by the passage of time, their struggle against obscurity remains a poignant reminder of the recurring cycle between opulence and plaintive cries for attention against its gilded backdrop.

Chapter 9: The Haymarket Affair – A Prelude to Rights

In the grand tableau of American history, where we elevate tales of entrepreneurial triumph and national fortitude, it is somewhat ironic how certain pivotal events remain both remembered and overlooked; prominent in the annals of infamy, yet strangely dismissed in their import. The Haymarket Affair is one such episode, a masterclass in the tome of tragic forewarnings—one might even call it a miniaturized Greek tragedy played out on the streets of Chicago.

On the fateful evening of May 4, 1886, a peaceful rally in Haymarket Square, advocating for the eight-hour workday, descended into chaos when an unexpected explosion pierced the night—a bomb hurled into the crowd, which resulted in the deaths of seven police officers and at least four civilians. The trial that followed was sensational, its flavor marked by a potent blend of judicial bias and public hysterics. Eight anarchists, mostly immigrants, were convicted not based on evidence of their guilt but on their beliefs, affiliations, and foreignness. How quaintly consistent of America, a nation of immigrants, to turn a blind eye to the complexities of its melting pot while supping from it.

This turbulent chapter exposes a narrative profoundly American in its duality: the perpetual struggle between capital and labor, immigrant anxieties, and the quest for civil liberties. Herein lies the crux of the irony; for as this explosive affair unfolded, it planted seeds for the labor movement that would not bear fruit until well into the next century. The Haymarket Affair was not merely a moment of violence; it was a clarion call, an early herald of the labor rights movement that would stir the American conscience, albeit at glacial speed.

Decades later, as the wheels of industry ground inexorably on, one might wonder how a nation that pledged allegiance to progress managed to overlook this early cry for worker dignity. The eight-hour workday, a concept so revolutionary at the time, is now enshrined in labor laws, a testament to those who dared to imagine a world not dominated by the endless grind. Yet, how slow we were to get there! The lesson proffered by Haymarket was conveniently stuffed away, only to be revisited when subsequent generations faced similar uprisings and agitations. It took further strikes, lockouts, and the eventual emergence of labor unions to shepherd meaningful reforms into existence.

Yet, there's a curious contradiction in how we recall this affair today—a time when irony is both a narrative device and an outlook of choice. In our march toward progress, the Haymarket Affair often serves as an historical footnote; a day laborers commemorate each May 1st, under the moniker of International Workers' Day, while many Americans associate the occasion with that quintessentially suburban holiday, Memorial Day, which celebrates the start of summer more robustly than worker's rights. Splendidly ironic, is it not, that the very seat of democratic ideals has marginalized a seminal event that underscores its citizens' collective struggle for equitable rights?

In revisiting the Haymarket Affair, we find ourselves trudging through layers of historical sediment, uncovering both the rawness of its immediate impact and the irony of its continued relevance. Though we have moved on from the discordant cacophony of an industrializing age, the underlying themes remain hauntingly contemporary: immigration, the rights of labor versus those of capital, and the search for balance between freedom and order.

As we stand on the precipice of 2025, engulfed in a reality where labor dynamics are once again shifting—fueled by the explosions of automation and globalization—one might muse over how little has changed. Where the Haymarket tumult once echoed with cries for the dignity of work and the humanity of its doers, we now observe laborers facing equally arduous battles over dignity, evidence that past lessons, though clear as day, are easily disregarded when inconvenient.

History, it seems, is stubbornly cyclical, a mirror reflecting our proclivity for forgetting its instructive echoes. The Haymarket Affair, rather than a dusty relic tethered to an antiquated past, emerges in this ironic retelling as both a harbinger and a poignant reminder: the march toward human rights, persistently beleaguered but unyielding, may be delayed—yet never denied.

Chapter 10: The Panic of 1893 – A Golden Collapse

The Panic of 1893 stands as a monument to the peculiarly American ability to transform boundless prosperity into profound despair. It is the era's crowning achievement in irony that, amid the glow of the Gilded Age—a time when society and economy alike were supposedly polished to a high sheen—a near-catastrophic economic collapse unceremoniously unraveled the fabric of ostentatious wealth. Beneath the glittering surface lay the harsh reality of financial instability, a striking phenomenon one might think we'd never see again. And yet, in a curiously repetitive dance, history has hummed similar tunes even as we've waltzed our way into 2025.

During the Gilded Age, the United States, decked out in its finest industrial regalia, experienced growth so staggering that it must have felt like some cosmic jest. Railroads crisscrossed the country, steel shot up into the skies, and spilling from the stockyards of Chicago were fortunes ambitious enough to rival the excesses of the pharaohs. Yet, beneath this shimmering façade lived a disorder that barely obscured the economic tremors ready to topple the precarious structure.

The Panic of 1893 began, as these things often do, with a chain reaction. The collapse of the Philadelphia and Reading Railroad was merely the first domino. With it fell a cascade of businesses and banks, resulting in an alarming distress signal: the callous clanging shut of the nation's vaults, where money-makers raucously celebrated innovation during daylight hours. By evening, however, they found themselves whispering prayers to escape bankruptcy's specter. In a single year, scores of banks closed, millions were thrust into joblessness, and the myth of infinite prosperity dissipated like smoke in the wind.

What is truly remarkable—and abundantly ironic—is how this scenario seemed destined to replay, with slight variants, throughout the 20th and into the 21st century. One almost admires the human capacity to brush against the thorns of financial collapse time and time again without appearing to learn from its sting. Lessons of the Panic seemed drowned in the zeal for more opulence and the irresistible seduction of speculation.

Fast forward to our contemporary times, where we find ourselves facing the challenges of digital currencies and market volatility, once again straddling that fine line between monumental wealth and economic fragility. The modern-day reflection of the Panic of 1893 presents itself in cryptocurrency crashes, sudden stock market falls, and unforeseen global financial crises that prove rather inconvenient for those who had begun to think stability had finally been achieved.

Like a gilded butterfly drawn enticingly close to an open flame, those pursuing wealth found themselves repeatedly consumed by the same luminous promise that had felled their ancestors. Surely, one would think, we of 2025 might have grasped the lessons from a golden collapse long past. Yet, here we are, marveling at our digital railroads, which, much like their 19th-century counterparts, occasionally reveal hidden cracks in their gleaming tracks.

Thus, the saga continues: a grand irony played out on the stage of human advancement. Where opulence lives, financial instability lurks nearby, lurking behind the curtain, waiting for its inevitable, dramatic entrance. The Panic of 1893 is a stark reminder, enshrined in its place in history, raising the pert question whether humankind learns less from success than from its failures—or whether it learns at all. If nothing else, this cyclical dance between prosperity and precariousness is a testament to the enduring, if bewildering, human determination to persist in hope, come feast or famine.

Chapter 11: Literature of the Gilded Age – The Pen's Irony

The Gilded Age, a period bursting with the gleam of prosperity and the shadowy depths of destitution, offered an irresistible tableau for the illustrious minds who dared to wield the pen. The writers of this era, chief among them being Mark Twain and Stephen Crane, immersed themselves in the scintillating chaos and emerged with works that both celebrated and castigated the grand absurdity that was late 19th-century America. Their literary prowess, remarked for its sharp irony and unflinching realism, transformed the written word into a mirror reflecting the manifold ironies of wealth and poverty.

Mark Twain, a veritable lion of letters, possessed a tongue-in-cheek style that blended humor with deep social critique. Through masterful works such as "The Gilded Age: A Tale of Today" and "Adventures of Huckleberry Finn," Twain laid bare the glaring contradictions of the era. The former, co-authored with Charles Dudley Warner, served as both a namesake and a seminal piece for this age of opulence and ostentation. With his characteristically sardonic wit, Twain dared to suggest that beneath the nation's gold-plated surface lay a foundation fragile and poorly constructed—a metaphor not simply for the economy, but also for the moral fabric of society itself.

"The Adventures of Huckleberry Finn," often hailed as a cornerstone of American literature, ventured where few were bold enough to tread. Twain's Huck Finn skewered the absurdity of societal norms and the grotesque spectacle of human prejudice. The great irony of Huck, an uneducated boy, possessing a moral compass more finely attuned than the so-called civilized adults, was not lost on Twain's astute readership. Moreover, the episodic journey along the Mississippi River unfurled a panorama of American life that exposed the cracks in the facade of prosperity. Twain's satire was dual-edged—both entertaining and unsettling—an invitation for readers to laugh while uncomfortably confronting themselves in the reflection.

Enter Stephen Crane, a literary figure whose realist narrative cut through the era's social pretense with surgical precision. Crane eschewed the familial bliss of "domestic fiction" for the unvarnished truth of man's struggle against the indifferent forces of nature and society. In his masterwork, "Maggie: A Girl of the

Streets," Crane vividly illustrated the brutal determinism of poverty, permitting no romantic delusions or gilded coverings to obscure the reader's view. With a touch as stark as an unswept tenement, he portrayed the irony of American dreams dashed against the harsh realities of urban existence.

Crane's ability to depict the human condition in its stark nakedness—without the embellishments of sentimentality—enhanced his narratives with an irony that asked incredulous questions of an audience comfortable in its collective amnesia. How could a society so blindly enamored with its new-found wealth allow the likes of Maggie to sink beneath the undertow of destitution unnoticed or unremarked? His stories, set against the gritty backdrop of New York, testified to the truth that progress and poverty were inextricably entangled bedfellows.

In their respective idioms, Twain and Crane delivered a one-two literary punch that reflected, with undeniable irony, the inverted domestic bliss of the Gilded Age. Twain, with his satirical flair, turned the American optimism of success on its head, delivering biting social commentary dressed in humor and adventure. Crane, conversely, stripped away the luxurious veneer to reveal the heartache lurking beneath—harsh and unyielding as the city's unforgiving streets.

Together, Twain and Crane represented divergent yet complementary perspectives that reshaped their era's narrative. They crafted a portrait of a nation emblazoned with a façade of grandeur, wherein the pen became mightier than the gilded edges of the age's riches. Their literary offerings invite us, even today, to gaze through the gilded frame into a picture of society seemingly arrested in time—fraught with irony, saturated with truth, and perpetually reflective of our own ongoing journey from opulence to 2025.

Chapter 12: The Long Goodbye – Transitioning to the Progressive Era

Ah, the Gilded Age, that remarkable epoch when America's glittering surface concealed an intricate tapestry of moral ambiguities and social paradoxes. An era replete with barons of industry and the paupers they "generously" employed, with all the warmth of an iron spike. It was a time when the ostentatious found comfort in their golden mansions while the huddled masses yearned for basic decency across the cobbled streets. But as the 19th century waned, a curious phenomenon began to unfurl—a collective realization that perhaps, just perhaps, the scales of justice had tipped a bit too far in one direction.

The Progressive Era, as it would come to be known, marked the commencement of a belated endeavor to balance these scales, a shift from the indulgent mirages of prosperity to something resembling equitable reality. Yet, let us not be overly hasty in celebrating the triumphs of progressivism. After all, the efforts of these well-intentioned reformers are often met with as much irony as the age they sought to conclude.

Our tale begins with an inevitable dissatisfaction. The laborers, who had borne the burden of America's opulent ascent on their weary backs, found voice, albeit faintly, in the rising cacophony for reform. Here lies the irony: the very foundation upon which the nation's wealth was built had become restless, demanding a share of the prosperity they had unintentionally fashioned. But do not be fooled; the road to justice was neither prompt nor smooth.

The call for systemic reform echoed across the nation, resonating in factories where safety was but an afterthought and in tenements where overcrowding made privacy a distant dream. Progressive champions, armed with pens and an earnest earnestness, advocated for the end of child labor and for women to have the audacity to vote. These reformers painted vivid pictures of a society where opportunity was not a privilege reserved for the few but a right accessible to all. Alas, in their haste, they occasionally forgot that entrenched structures of power rarely welcome change with open arms.

Consider the plight of the muckrakers, those intrepid journalists who charged into the depths of America's industrial heart, wielding words like finely honed daggers. Their work revealed truths that had long skulked in the shadows: corruption woven into political tapestries, corporate malfeasance hiding beneath respectable veneers, and the pervasive exploitation that tarnished the promise of the American Dream. But, as one might wryly observe, exposing the rot is a world away from eradicating it.

The push for reform culminated in landmark legislations, fleeting victories that served as mere stepping stones in a vastly undetermined journey. The Pure Food and Drug Act of 1906 and the establishment of the Federal Reserve System did signal incremental progress. Yet they also underscored the irony of a society striving to legislate behavior it had so carefully nurtured.

Let us also not overlook the nuanced dance between the states and federal power. Many progressive reformers learned, to their chagrin, that while laws may be enacted, their enforcement often lagged, ensnared in bureaucracies and political reluctance. A cynic might suggest that while the heart longs for reform, the hand often lingers, perhaps pondering the cost of compliance.

Indeed, as this chapter closes, we must acknowledge that the transition from the Gilded Age to the Progressive Era was neither swift nor linear. It was a period marked by paltry triumphs wrestled from the jaws of adversity, propelled by individuals and movements insisting on the necessity of reform, even as the status quo clung to its well-worn path.

And so, with a measure of irony, we bid farewell to the Gilded Age, a grandly extravagant epoch bustling with ambition and avoidance alike. The dawn of the Progressive Era beckoned a nation toward a more equitable future, a journey still unfolding in the shadow of history's not-so-distant gilded mirage. As progressives charted the course for systemic reform and justice, they also revealed the persistent truth: the road to righteousness is often paved with good intentions and uneasy ironies.

PART II

Echoes of the Gilded Age in 2025 – A Familiar Melody

Chapter 13: The Second Coming – Economic Reverberations of 2025

It would appear that history has a particular affinity for repeating itself, much like a favorite symphony doomed to echo repeatedly across the concert halls of time. In this iteration of the great opera that is human progress, the economic scene of 2025 has draped itself in the decadence and disparity reminiscent of the storied Gilded Age. Once again, wealth has donned its shiny mask and played out its sordid theater on the world stage. However, in the grandeur of this new act, technology now shares the limelight, imbuing the narrative with both awe and irony.

The Gilded Age—a time when industrial barons carved empires from steel and smoke—has found its spiritual successor in the digital titans of our era. Names such as Zuckerberg, Musk, and Bezos now echo with the same gravitas once reserved for Rockefeller, Carnegie, and Vanderbilt. Their industries may differ, but the allegory is strikingly familiar. The present technological renaissance has cultivated innovation at an unprecedented pace, much as the railways and factories once did, yet the fruits of this harvest remain tantalizingly out of reach for the masses who toil to tend it.

In the gripping year of 2025, our economic hierarchy stands as a testament to high-wire acts perfected through centuries of practice. The top echelons of society float skyward, held aloft by helium-filled purses straining against the Earth's gravity. Meanwhile, the underbelly of society gazes upward, hoping their hard work will become a ladder rather than an empty promise. The digital divide—once merely a crack, presently a chasm—has paradoxically brought both hope and despair to the collective consciousness.

Artificial intelligence and automation have become the laureates of labor, delivering efficiency that would have left our industrial forebearers swooning in disbelief. Manufacturing, transportation, healthcare, and even social services have been revolutionized beyond recognition, blessing humanity with newfound capabilities. However, nestled within this digital utopia, a peculiar irony festers: for every job elevated by a silicon savior, another is rendered untouchable by human grasp. The promised utopia from whence technology emergences occasionally grins disturbingly akin to a dystopia.

As we continue to immerse ourselves in this new digital landscape, we cannot but marvel at the notion that access to knowledge, once a luxury, is now a commodity ripe for exploitation. The skyscrapers of cyberspace, though offering vistas never before witnessed, come with tolls no less onerous than those that crowded the paths of our railroad predecessors. The unbridled access to information serves as a currency in its own right—a currency found abundantly in what companies fittingly term "data." In a brazen twist of fate, privacy has become a plaything in the age of visibility, an ironic footnote in our quest for digital dominion.

Yet, these brilliant spectacles of irony are punctuated by moments of genuine progress. The same technologies widening our socioeconomic rift have ushered in advancements in medicine, education, and renewable energy. The promise of virtual classrooms allows learning without borders, just as renewable technologies tease a future less burdened by the chains of nonrenewable tyranny. Herein lies the paradox: in attempting to bridge the gap, these same tools wield the power to deepen the divide.

In 2025, we find ourselves fellow travelers upon a gossamer wire, suspended precariously between gleaming prosperity and somber reflection. The promise that technology embodies is palpable—far-reaching potential hinted at tantalizingly on the horizon. Yet, we must dare ask whether the gilded luster that cloaks this era conceals a rusting core. The Second Coming of the Gilded Age, armed with silicon and code, beckons forth an era both dazzling and daunting. As the world continues to pirouette on this razor's edge, one must ponder whether history's great symphony, clad in irony, has more verses yet unsung.

Chapter 14: Modern-Day Moguls – The Tech Titans

As we delve into the 21st century's iteration of the Gilded Age, we are obliged to suspend disbelief in marveling at the new breed of moguls who dominate the modern era. These illustrious figures—Jeff Bezos, Mark Zuckerberg, and Elon Musk—are not wrought in the image of Carnegie or Rockefeller, their empires not forged from the tangible world of steam and steel. Instead, they exist in a landscape constructed largely from bits, bytes, and broadband—an empire of zeros and ones heralded as the new cornerstone of commerce and communication.

Jeff Bezos, for instance, ostensibly emerged from humble beginnings. His genius was spotting that a digital bookshop could morph into a global colossus, selling everything from literature to lingerie. Amazon, once an emblematic disruptor of the retail book industry, now materializes as a kind of omnipotent deity of consumer culture. With a mere click or swipe, an array of goods materializes at the doorstep, as if by magic. Bezos himself, with his rakish smile and shaven head, grinned widely atop the list of the world's wealthiest for years. And who could blame him? After all, one must have a firm grip on reality to send oneself to space on a phallic-shaped rocket named Blue Origin—an apt monument to his magnitude, subtlety notwithstanding.

Next, let us turn our ironic gaze to Mark Zuckerberg, the harbinger of humanity's social revolution. Having inadvertently designated himself as the modern oracle of interpersonal interaction, Zuckerberg's legacy lies enshrined in the digital halls of Facebook—or Meta, as he envisioned a rebranded metaverse future as infinite as it is speculative. Advancing the idea that we should connect more deeply by interacting through avatars than in genuine tactile company, Zuckerberg offers a novel form of intimacy free from the messiness of, well, actual human beings. How poetic that a platform devised in a Harvard dormitory has grown to influence the public discourse with the precision of a sledgehammer and finesse of a freight train.

And finally, we cannot omit Elon Musk, the enfant terrible of technology, whose taste for the eccentric matches his appetite for innovation. Where others saw barriers, Musk envisioned bold new worlds. Shall we commute to Mars, boring tunnels beneath our cities as easily as digging into a backyard garden? Musk says, "Why not?" His Tesla endeavor has reinvented electric cars, and then some, capturing the public's imagination with autopilot dreams and aspirations to surveil the stars from vehicles costlier than the average home. His Twitter escapades, meanwhile, serve as a continuous reminder of his whimsical lever toward digital expression—often blending the lines between genius and folly with astonishing frequency.

Of course, each titan stands as a paragon of his own brand of success, and none would dare deny the economic ripples their empires have caused. Yet, within their stories resonates a certain irony. These titans operate under the banner of transformational visionaries but often seem to reconstruct the same paradigms they claim to dismantle—consolidating power, hoarding wealth, and at times, eclipsing ethical standards in their march towards progress.

In this ironic reflection of human enterprise, these modern-day moguls have redefined wealth and power through digital constructs, transforming society even as they mirror the ambitions of their 19th-century predecessors. The question remains: as the age advances forward, what legacy will these titans leave?

Will their empires stand the test of time, or will they, too, crumble like gilded constructs of past glories? Only time will tell if these digital magnates can sustain their ascent or if their lofty ambitions will succumb to virtual decay. Until then, marvel we must, at the digital empires upon whose silicon foundations the future awaits to be built—or perhaps, unraveled.

Chapter 15: Innovation for the Few – Tech's Golden Curtain

The Gilded Age was an era of startling opulence and stark inequality, but history shows that human ingenuity knows no bounds when it comes to leaving some behind. As we gather in 2025 to revisit that age, it's with a nod to the unparalleled irony of our circumstances: the cutting-edge technologies that were supposed to democratize opportunity have instead become a dazzling curtain obscuring the growing chasm between those who lead and those who simply follow.

Ah, the intoxicating lure of innovation! Behold the wizardry of 3D-printed organs, quantum computing, and artificial intelligence shimmering like high-wattage beacons of modern progress. Who could have imagined that such wonders would materialize only for a select group with the foresight—or perhaps just the fortune—of geography and social standing? It seems, after all, that the great promise of technology was not to propel us all unto a Utopian horizon, but to furnish a golden curtain that separates the tech-savvy elite from the haplessly marooned.

Indeed, the once-revolutionary ideas of connectivity and access have become yet another echelon of privilege. The Digital Divide now feels like a quaint relic compared to the Grand Canyon it has become. Those few at the pantheon of Silicon Valley feast not only on organic kale but on data, reaped from devices that beckon to the rest of the world like sirens guiding ships to shore and only to founders who stand on islands of plenty.

Do not mistake this as a lament; it is an era of splendid times, indeed—for those who hold the keys to the digital kingdom. Venture capitalists clink glasses over investments in the latest deep tech while pondering ways to skyrocket to Mars, as the gold-plated treasures of innovation sift down to them like manna from an imagined heaven. Meanwhile, their employees don virtual headsets to escape the reality these technologies have conveniently obscured—their roles as mere cogs in a well-oiled, finely-tuned machine designed for someone else's gain.

For those who found themselves on this golden curtain's tragicomic Stage Left, the illumination of their screens is a pale reflection of lost promise, an eerie glow that fills living rooms but not with light. Connectivity, that supposed panacea to social disparity, manifests itself as endless scrolls and video streams that only deepen the sense of alienation—ambient lights flickering from screens crowded with advertisements, each whispering of a lifestyle just out of reach.

In a world ever more reliant on the bits and bytes coursing through fiber optics, the skills necessary to ascend this golden ladder remain a rarefied commodity. The educational institutions tout progressivism, offering courses that glisten with buzzwords like "disrupt," "innovate," and "blockchain," yet they are accessible predominantly to those who can afford them—the same few whose paths never impinge on the frontiers of obsolescence. The others, they sift through free online courses and piecemeal knowledge, ever hopeful of building a bridge across the divide that continues widening under the weight of their aspirations.

Further irony plays out in burgeoning debates on tech ethics and sustainability, primarily held within circles barricaded from those questions' darkest implications. We marvel at the latest carbon-neutral invention while other hands in distant lands disassemble yesterday's electronics—our discarded dreams—among toxic ruins in the name of survival.

In this new gilded age, we beg the question: Is innovation an agent of change, or a portrait of irony, as masterfully wrought as any by da Vinci, nonetheless leaving the observer eternally apart from the artistry? For, after all, while the curtain remains alluringly luminous, its folds imperviously dense, draping the future in a dichotomy of brilliance and shadow.

Let history judge if it was our triumph or our folly that painted such a remarkable but ruthlessly selective picture of progress. As the world spins to the humming cadence of server farms and data streams, we can perhaps only hope the loudest note played is not of futility but of awakening. Wouldn't that be the ultimate innovation—a world where the curtain finally rises for all? Until then, admire the sheen, if you can.

Chapter 16: Labor's New Voice – A Gig Economy Reality**

In the dazzling dawn of the Gilded Age, the clangor of industry reverberated across America, a siren call for prosperity and progress. But beneath this symphonic surge lay the staccato cries of the labor force—voices hitherto marginalized, whose crescendo would soon demand attention. Fast forward to the digital renaissance of the 21st century, and one would assume that history's lessons were etched into the moral fabric of society. Alas, the unfolding tale bears a familiar plot, replete with the cacophony of divided realities.

As we thrust into the age of tech-induced euphoria, a pantheon of innovation deified by the masses, emerged the gig economy—a realm promising the liberation of choice, autonomy, and a departure from draconian office confines. Optimistic evangelists heralded this shift as the inevitable evolution towards utopian labor. Yet, lo and behold, within this gilded framework resides a parallel narrative, unrecited by the automated bards: the gig workers' plight—a subdued echo of yesteryear's laborers whose cries had seemingly been archived under 'lessons learned.'

In an ironic twist of fate, these modern laborers, or "independent contractors" as corporate lexicon ordained, found themselves ensnared in an eerily reminiscent cycle of volatility and disenfranchisement. Just as it was with the factory hands of old, whose plight was eloquently overshadowed by the jubilation of mechanized advancement, today's digital laborers toil in obscurity—hidden beneath layers of codified algorithms and monetized platforms. Their voices, much like phantom whispers in the digital corridor, encounter a society more enamored with the glimmers of gadgetry and innovation than with the uneasy whispers of inequality.

The irony lies not only in the echo, but in the evolution; or, dare I say, the stagnation of discernment. With technological melodies rapturously twinkling in every connected home, who would notice the muted chorus of dissent? In an epoch where the latest device garners more communal celebration than the welfare of its enablers, the question begged is one of societal priorities and collective amnesia.

Gig work, much like its industrial predecessor, was championed as a boon of flexibility. "Work when you want, as much as you want," sang the digital sirens. But for many, this song tethers them to an ever-elusive promise, where the harmony between aspiration and reality is dissonant at best. Irregular hours, inconsistent income, and non-existent benefits characterize this neo-feudal existence, where the autonomy heralded is often the autonomy to struggle.

Despite this, the indomitable spirit of labor endures. Organizing in digital forums—today's answer to the union halls of old—gig workers unite. Whispered grievances evolve into shouted demands for basic rights, hopes rekindled by the faint yet persistent fires of collective action. Their defiance, a testament to human resilience, is a poignant reminder that even amidst the most daunting epochs, labor's voice finds new dynamics.

In closing this ironic reflection, one cannot help but ponder the cyclical nature of society's engagement with labor. As innovation continues its restless march forward, might we dare to dream of a future where progress and prosperity accommodate the very architects of their edifices? Let history not repeat as mere parody but evolve, directing its lessons towards empathic advancement. Can we truly evolve beyond the gilded illusions of progress to recognize the enduring worth of every worker's contribution? One can only hope.

Chapter 17: The Socialite Revival – Redefining Opulence

In the annals of history, the Gilded Age endures as a beacon of extravagance—an era of intimate soirées, burgeoning skyscrapers, and fortunes amassed overnight. Yet, as we saunter through the corridors of time, it's abundantly clear that the spirit of opulence didn't dissolve with the glow of gaslight. Instead, it has shapeshifted into new forms, as if echoing Oscar Wilde's sentiment that nothing succeeds like excess.

Gone are the days when Miss Eliza Vanderplume would curtsy in frothy lace at the cotillion ball, signaling her official induction into society's upper echelons. In this era of digital whims, her modern counterpart wields a smartphone, broadcasting real-time glamour as a luxury influencer. Though less bound by societal etiquette than her debutante foremothers, she embodies a new form of meticulous curation. Her visage is equally as groomed; her wardrobe surpasses any diamond-festooned tiara, replaced by a calculated curation of 'haute' moments that speak to a globally tuned-in audience. Illustrating, once again, that the more things change, the more they remain ostentatiously the same.

The modern narrative of opulence is written not in the dusty ledgers of trade barons but on Instagram grids and TikTok uploads. Private jets and sprawling estates still play their roles, yet their purpose evolves with the flicker of an LED screen. Instead of whispering about stock portfolios in smoky parlors, today's elite engage in conspicuous displays of consumption available for public dissection and adoration. Economic depreciation aside, the private island vacation is not truly enjoyed unless documented and hashtagged. For what is wealth if not affirmed by the anonymous applause of millions?

The irony, perhaps, is the wonderfully democratic nature of this exhibitionist oligarchy; each iPhone bearing witness concedes a peculiar empowerment to both observer and observed. Where the Gilded Age's aristocracy shielded itself behind gates and drapes of exclusivity, the contemporary avatar proudly parades before the world, insisting by mere existence, that boundary between common man and platformed paragon has been erased—or at least wildly blurred.

And let us not forget how tech billionaires—our modern industrial titans—play in this grand spectacle. Slightly more tech-savvy than their Gilded predecessors but no less theatrical, they are the benefactors and purveyors of our age's grand balls: where code and capital entwine to stream endless euphoria or angst, delivered daily onto our glowing screens. In revealing the vastness of their affluence, they court public fascination and sometimes ire, thus validating their supremacy in our post-industrial society. How enchanting!

In this world, opulence manifests not just in garish possessions but in the currency of experiences—the more exclusive and inaccessible, the better. Culinary fêtes curated by Michelin-star chefs, attended by select socialites flown in rather than born into the scene, transcend any belle époque gala's grandeur. Yet perhaps it's not just the wealth on display but the well-choreographed narrative of spontaneity that truly dazzles. That any viewer could embark on similar ventures, if not for a small matter of several zeros.

Still, beneath this conspicuous hedonism lies the ever-present irony of our peculiar zeitgeist: the more we attempt to democratize luxury through virtual lenses, the more we realize that lived experience remains maddeningly, insultingly stratified. The gilded palaces may have transformed into penthouses and algorithms, but the tapestry of luxury maintains its timeless sheen—a scrim through which we glimpse glimpses, contradicting the larger disconnect.

As we survey today's socialite revival, one cannot help but smirk at the continuation of this unbroken thread of grandeur—a testament to humanity's perennial pursuit of opulence, social stratification, and the tools through which we manifest them. With each post and repost, the cycle perpetuates itself in our irony-steeped modernity; a dance as symphonic and elaborate as any waltz across a grand old ballroom floor, spinning into the future. The stage is set, the players—both new and old—remain keenly aware of their audience. So let's raise a glass, perhaps not of champagne but of filtered alchemy, to this new gilded performance in all its splendid absurdity.

Chapter 18: Political Theatre Redux – Lobbyists and their Legislators

In an era touted as one of unprecedented progress and technological marvel—because, after all, what is a century without its personal renaissance—the modern blend of governance and corporate interests continues to delight the discerning spectator of political theatre. The complex and harmonious choreography of lobbyists and legislators vibrantly reaffirm that some performances, the most elemental ones, stand unwavering in the drafts of time.

Picture this: A grand stage whereupon the architects of policy and profit engage in a delicate duet, each move precisely orchestrated, each note perfectly attuned to the chords of influence and aspiration. This affair is anything but ordinary; it is democracy in its most refined and evolved form or, perhaps, simply the most lucrative form of tradition. For it seems that the gilding of the age still gleams, no matter how often it is wiped, and certainly, the play must go on.

As it turns out, the art of lobbying—a term that invites polite chuckles or bemused sighs—is no mere supporting act but rather the lead role in this spectacle that is contemporary politics. Detractors might argue the term "public servant" feels ever-so-slightly outdated when self-interest masquerades with altruistic airs. Yet, how fortunate we are to witness each meticulously crafted overture that negotiates and navigates through the corridors of power, blending vested interest with public service in such beautifully beneficial ways.

The lobbyists, those directors of ambition, have seemingly mastered a craft that transforms simple legislation into a fine-tuned symphony, resplendent with the soothing harmonies of capital persuasion. With expertise that rivals Renaissance virtuosos, they pivot and pirouette through complex choreography, ensuring that no influential player on the cold stone floor of governance is left unturned or, indeed, unimpressed. Their agendas, veiled as concerted efforts for collective good, promise that growth, innovation, and prosperity find their rightful place in the sun—though who benefits most from this gleaming warmth is a revelation best left to the shadows.

Enter the legislators, as dedicated thespians whose roles require the utmost dexterity. They must possess the rare ability to cast parts of earnest idealists and seasoned negotiators simultaneously, convincing audiences of their unwavering dedication to the people's welfare while assuring beneficiaries of their strategic alignments. Such is the modern role of governance—so appropriately attuned to embrace the evolving script of political realities without ever deviating from the ultimate encore: re-election, perchance, or a more corporately gilded retirement.

In a familiar tradition, the revolving doors that belonged to earlier ages open with predictable yet compelling intrigue. Bids of influence add texture to the already rich tapestry of governance in the 21st-century democratic spirit. Once critical of industry power-brokers, we now watch appreciatively as regulators become regulated, allowing the symbiosis between public office and private enterprise to blossom with indistinguishable boundaries. Indeed, it would be an oversight not to acknowledge the flair of continuity in an otherwise unpredictable landscape.

Thus, basking under the spotlight, the theatrics of governance continue to thrive, echoing the performative elements that endeared a simpler, albeit jeweler's version, of this dance to our forebears more than a century ago. "Meet the new boss," as they say—who may well be that board member you endorsed last quarter or entertained last night. In splendid irony, they remain casually acquainted, deeply entwined, and unchanged.

As the curtains fall, that grand stage of political theatre reveals itself as far less lofty than conceived—a plateau intricately crafted with economic opportunity and ideological seasoning, diverse professions of future promise delivered in unwavering cadence. After all, it is a legacy willingly embraced, a tour de force that history and destiny eagerly conspire to sustain. Ultimately, the opulence and ambition symbolized in this ever-spinning production continue to invite both adulation and critique, ensuring that we're always, just as attentively, inching toward the next revival with baited breath.

Chapter 19: Metropolis Redux – Tech Hubs and the Urban Divide

Ah, Silicon Valley—a veritable shrine of glass and steel, where innovation promises to lift humanity to celestial heights. One can almost taste the pixels in the air, a tantalizing aroma of success! The valley's high-rises, boasting architectural designs that blur the lines between science fiction and reality, stand as monuments to human ingenuity. In these hallowed halls of innovation, new gods are born: algorithms, data sets, and digital currencies, each promising to liberate us from the gravity of our mundane existence. Yet, irony laughs silently in the shadows, for at the feet of these towers lie the sprawling encampments of the less fortunate—a testament to a different sort of ingenuity, one where survival itself is an act of daily innovation.

Here, in the heart of technological transcendence, the promise of a digital utopia is eclipsed by the harsh reality of increasing urban squalor. The Valley's meteoric ascent has summoned an unlikely neighbor—homelessness, clad in tents and tarpaulins, staking a claim on the sidewalks designed for prosperity. It is a peculiarly modern tapestry, this juxtaposition of opulence and deprivation, where electric scooters slalom around makeshift dwellings and low-orbit satellites twinkle with the possibility of universal Wi-Fi for all, including those who can scarcely afford a loaf of bread. A desolate beauty, indeed, in the gentrification that claims to bestow value upon the land while systematically eroding the very soul of community.

The urban divide in Silicon Valley symbolizes a broader phenomenon encroaching upon metropolises worldwide—a division of realities stark enough to make even a Dickensian narrative blush with its brazenness. The gilded high-rises, shimmering in the Californian sun, house the privileged few, sheltered by their digital cocoons against the pandemonium of the outside world. Inside, everything exudes calm and order, punctuated by the hum of servers and robotic processes that ensure tasks are executed with mechanical precision. The irony is as glistening as the structures themselves: the very platforms that promised to unite the world have instead fostered islands of luxury, separated by a sea of disparity.

Let us wander, now, through the streets of the metropolis that promise opportunity for all but deliver it selectively. Here innovation thrives, not merely as acts of technological advancement but also in the social stratagems employed by those on the margins of society. While some innovate their way to million-dollar IPOs, others, without shelter, innovate survival: constructing makeshift homes with discarded cardboard and plastic, curating a semblance of privacy amidst the relentless exposure of street life. Yet, as the urban landscape warps into digital utopias for the select few, a question persists, profound in its simplicity: how can systems built on innovations for the future forget those who desperately need change in the present?

In the boardrooms perched high above the city, power suits discuss the future with a sense of manicured urgency. Unbeknownst to them—or perhaps known, yet unacknowledged—a different kind of meeting convenes below: a congregation forged by necessity, strategizing the night's shelter or the day's meal. Remarkably, these concurrent meetings may discuss similar topics, albeit with different stakes: security, resources, and connectivity. How fascinating it is to observe the labyrinth of bureaucracy, where local governments wrestle with gargantuan enterprises over taxes while municipal services groan under the weight of the disenfranchised seeking solace on their streets.

So it is in these urban crucibles, celebrated for their intellectual might and technical wizardry, that the irony of the modern epoch unfolds—a melodrama between human privilege and poverty, both clinging fiercely to the promise of progress. Silly, isn't it, that in a world capable of raising skyscrapers to honor the likes of binary code, we hesitate to bridge the tangible, yawning gaps between people? Perhaps this is the most intricate algorithm of all—the perennial question of coexistence in the shadow of genius and the glow of prosperity.

As night falls, the valley dons its coat of twinkling lights, an image almost poetic in its serenity. Yet, the darkness also cloaks the reality below, a teeming bed of contradictions that no mere wealth or welfare check can easily resolve. Perhaps the greatest irony of our age is that in the thrumming heart of progress, where dreams are incubated and ideas take flight, we still struggle to harmonize the quest for more with the ancient, simple wish of dignity for all. Yes, Silicon Valley—a complex testament to the human condition: an opulent dystopia and a hopeful elegy, all wrapped into one.

Chapter 20: Rural Voices Rise – Echoes of Farmer Populism

In the landscape of American history, where skyscrapers scrape the heavens and hollow steel embodies triumph, the rural heartland whispers—no, roars—under the sheer pressure of neglect. The Gilded Age, that era of unparalleled opulence, showcased a nation divided not merely by economic stratifications, but by an ironic tapestry of progress woven alongside deeply ingrained injustices. While urban magnates reveled in their resplendent towers of steel and greed, another narrative quietly seethed across the fields and farms: that of farmer populism, resonating with a fervor that refused to be silenced.

As industrialization marched forward with the blind arrogance of a conqueror, the American farmer was left to till not just the soil, but a growing sense of disillusionment. Despite the bucolic depictions painted in the parlors of power, agriculture was not the quaint backbone of a pastoral dream, but a battlefield of economic survival. The farmer, burdened by debt, falling prices, and a capricious market, became the overlooked casualty in the nation's relentless chase for progress. Herein lies the supreme irony: while cities burgeoned under the cloak of prosperity, the rural heartland echoed with cries that refused to harmonize with the oblivious serenade of the Gilded Age's ruling elite.

These cries, however, soon found a voice—a movement that billowed forth like the very dust from plowed fields. Farmer populism, with its roots entrenched in real hardship and communal perseverance, emerged not as a mere protest, but as a clarion call for equity and fairness. The People's Party, born from the frustrations of the Farmer's Alliance, sought to lift the veil of indifference, demanding reforms that would unshackle the agrarian community from the chains of exploitation. Railroads, these iron veins of commerce, were accused of bleeding the farmer dry with exorbitant freight rates, while financial institutions tightened their grip with crippling interest rates. The populists' platform was a mosaic of democratic ideals, poignantly simple, and brazenly radical: to reclaim power for the people, to wrestle control from the plutocrats, and to bridge the growing chasm between the urban and rural.

Among the platforms they championed was the subtreasury plan—a rather novel idea proposing government warehouses where crops could be stored in exchange for loans, enabling farmers to sell on their own terms. Also challenged were the entrenched gold standards with a cry for bimetallism, seeking to inflate currency and ease the debt burden that pressed heavily on rural constituencies. Of course, the genteel city financiers, those paragons of economic wisdom cloistered in metropolitan towers, dismissed these solutions as economic naiveté. Oh, the irony of lecturing balance to those already teetering at the edge of subsistence!

Yet, despite the almost prophetic fervor with which populist leaders championed the cause, mainstream politicians continued to infuse their rhetoric with sympathy while draining it of substance. The movement's high-noon came with the tempestuous words of William Jennings Bryan, whose passionate "Cross of Gold" speech at the Democratic National Convention of 1896 became the emblematic battle cry of the populist cause. And while the words rang true within the hall, outside it met a world steeled by the complacency of success—a world for whom reform was, at best, a poetic reverie.

As decades blurred, the rural landscape evolved, echoing still with populist defiance, albeit often overshadowed by the cacophony of urban progress. Mechanization whispered promises of reprieve; subsidies dangled like sterile tokens of affection from a disconnected government. Yet, even as the world trundles towards 2025, the legacy of farmer populism endures, a recurring tension that resuscitates itself whenever whispers of neglect swell into voices of dissent.

Today, policymakers, clad in suits tailored to perfection, sit in climate-controlled offices designing rural American futures—a rich irony that echoes the past. They discuss sustainable agriculture over catered luncheons and extol digital connectivity to areas where sometimes even water struggles to find its way. Rural America may occasionally find itself wrapped in a swathe of digitalization, but its heart still beats in rhythm with an older melody—the call for recognition, for partnership, for genuine consideration.

In the grand mosaic of American history, the farmer remains an intricate motif. And herein lies the greatest irony: modernity may have airbrushed away his struggles, but the echoes of farmer populism continue to resonate, stubbornly refusing to be mere footnotes to progress. The farmer's plight, once disregarded, holds deep within it the lesson modern powers still fail to wholly heed—a vibrant reminder that within every gilded age lies the humblest of cries, waiting to be acknowledged.

Chapter 21: Protest and Pushback – Modern-Day Labor Movements

As the global tapestry of the new millennium began to unravel, its threads laid bare the unexpected continuity of a tale as old as industry itself. The chapter we now embroach nods to the familiar cadence of labor's cry— a clarion call of history playing out once more, though with a new digital twist. The 2020s saw the embodiment of this storied struggle not on the factory floor, but on platforms once relegated to the sharing of cat videos and vacation selfies. Welcome to protest and pushback made manifest in the ironic theater of social media.

From the guilds of medieval Europe to the factory hands of the Industrial Revolution, labor movements have long been the pulse of social change. Enter the digital age, and we find that these battlegrounds for fairness and dignity have simply changed their terrain. In a world where memes often speak louder than manifestos, the modern-day labor movement enjoys an oddly fitting platform on social media, where irony, like, share, and retweet perform the dual role of currency and soapbox.

The characters, though clad in the contemporary garb of avatars and hashtags, are but echoes of those who came before. Witness the app-based pilgrim, traversing the gig economy, finding refuge in virtual commons to exchange stories of overwork and underpay. It's a page out of the old playbooks, albeit with Wi-Fi. Social media, with its fickle allegiance and insatiable appetite for the trending, becomes the grand stage where grievances transform into viral movements, performing production after production in the theater of the absurd.

Take, for instance, the rise of the virtual collective of disgruntled warehouse workers. With the strike no longer solely a physical assembly, manifesting instead as a coordinated campaign of digital advocacy, one could argue that hashtags, in their ephemeral existence, have morphed into a digital picket line. Hearthside discussions and pamphlets have evolved into threads and live streams, where global audiences can tune in and offer their ephemeral support, clicking empathetically from the comfort of ergonomic chairs.

Consider the irony: workers' rights renaissance draws more engagement than any corporate performance review or institutional promise. The ubiquitous blue light of smartphones—emblems of our age of distraction—now pierces through digital fog to focus attention on labor inequities. The likes, shares, and comments become a new kind of ballot, one that is both immediate and yet perpetually under threat of being buried under the clutter of the internet's relentless churn.

With social platforms doubling as news outlets, the savviest labor movements employ the language of bytes and bandwidth. They leverage their visibility to reach lawmakers and boardrooms otherwise barricaded behind layers of red tape and bureaucracy. These digital foot soldiers speak in succinct quips and GIFs, utilizing brevity with mischievous reverence for ally-galvanizing and power-challenging.

And yet, no reflection—ironic or otherwise—would be complete without acknowledging the double-edged nature of this digital stage. Beneath the veneer of connectivity lies a lamentable reality: the attention spans that engage in labor advocacies are as fleeting as the virality they leverage. Like the 24-hour news cycle, the social media timeline hungers always for novelty, the cost of which is the diminution of sustained focus on any single issue. The worker's fight, which once simmered in factory towns for years, now risks being reduced to a fleeting blip on the digital radar.

The irony culminates in the sight of conglomerates themselves partaking in this modern theatrics. Employing social media campaigns that champion sustainability and ethical labor practices, these corporations craft images of allyship so artfully misaligned with reality that they almost perfect the postmodern pastiche. The workers fight not only for wages and hours but against the silhouettes of their simulacra as well.

And so, the tale winds its way through the digital marches and cybernetic sit-ins, perpetually reminding us of that age-old mantra, "The more things change, the more they stay the same." We find ourselves at a confluence of historic reprise and contemporary innovation—of avatars shouting cries of solidity into the void, where voicelessness was once the norm. This arena may be virtual, artifice and irony its currency, but the demand remains fervently real: justice, visibility, and voice.

Perhaps the ultimate irony, then, is this: in our age of infinite connectivity, the distance between a worker's plea and impactful change has never seemed wider, and yet, with each tap and click, we draw inexorably nearer.

Chapter 22: Financial Deja Vu – The Boom-Bust Cycle Returns

Ah, the Boom-Bust Cycle: a natural phenomenon as reliable as the moon's phases or the rising of the sun. To suggest it is merely a recurring event is an understatement; it is the beating heart of our economic tradition. Indeed, we find ourselves amid a financial panorama that would make the titans of the original Gilded Age nod in solemn recognition. They were masters of wealth creation and, equally, of wealth obliteration—a precarious dance that modern financiers have not only adopted but perfected.

The 21st century ushered in innovations that promised to break the chain of financial turmoil: economic models that could predict downturns, regulations to prevent reckless speculation, and algorithms designed to steer us clear of precipices. Yet, if history teaches us anything, it's our incapacity to learn from it. In a turn of events that would elicit wry grins from J.P. Morgan himself, the present mirrors the past—not as a distant echo but a booming declaration.

In the year 2025, we find ourselves on the familiar precipice of financial exuberance tempered by an equally familiar collapse. Stock portfolios soar to vertiginous heights, driven by industries grounded in digital realms and speculative assets so abstract they almost seem to defy gravity and common sense. Cryptocurrencies— those enigmatic strings of code— have rallied the new wave of tech-enthusiasts into a tizzy reminiscent of the tulip mania of centuries past. Enter said enthusiasts, believing fervently in their mythical immunity to economic despair, only to confront the sobering reality that volatility, like mischief, knows no generational bounds.

The irony of modern financial crises lies not in their inevitability but in their predictability. Each generation, armed with the unyielding confidence of youth, ventures into realms of speculation, believing they possess insights beyond the grasp of their predecessors. This audacious hubris, while undoubtedly invigorating, inevitably guides them toward the same cataclysmic pitfalls trodden by their forebears. And so, as the screens blink red and portfolios dwindle, a new cohort earns its stripes in the age-old rite of passage known as the financial crash.

However, it's too simplistic to dismiss these cycles as mere folly. The boom-bust rhythm, despite its chaos, is a spectacularly robust mechanism for one particular aspect: regenerative innovation. Every collapse cleanses the economic landscape, pruning the excesses and misjudgments of the preceding exuberance. From the ashes of each downfall—be it the railroad bankruptcies of the 19th century, the dot-com collapse of the early 21st, or the cryptocurrency wrecks of today—emerges a new order, paradoxically strengthened by prior miscalculations.

Yet, it's essential to note that this cycle of destruction and rebirth is not met equitably across society. While those nestled in ivory towers may bemoan market fluctuations in quaint parlors over scotches, these financial tremors ripple outward, reaching those least prepared to endure them—the everyday citizens whose lives hinge precariously on salaries and small investments. As headlines announce the latest overnight bankruptcies, it resonates like an old, haunting tune: "Another Speculative Bubble Bursts, Millions Affected."

So here we stand, poised at the edge of yet another fluctuation, with corporate esprits seeking fresh synergies and mergers, and financial juggernauts buying low in familiar, calculated precision. Venture capitalists, unfazed by short-term decimations, fund nascent ideas born from economic collapse—the very ideations that will inflate the next bubble. The cycle, omnipresent and unyielding, continues unabated.

In reflecting on this oddly reassuring dance of progress, or lack thereof, one can't help but appreciate the ironic symmetry of it all. Like actors bound to perform the same play over the decades, each new cast finds itself performing an age-old script with unfailing fidelity. And as the curtain rises on this latest act of our interminable economic saga, one truth remains eternal: every generation is destined to relearn the lessons of financial caution, discovering only in hindsight the adage that overconfidence precedes adversity.

Thus, we resign to embrace our modernity with a punctuated sense of déjà vu. Where once was rail, steel, and coal, now thrives tech stocks and cryptocurrency; the actors change, but the acts remain much the same. And so, we mill on toward the inevitable crescendo, fully aware that even in the age of omnipotent AI and economic savvy, we've yet made no greater an advancement over the ghosts of the past than a keener appreciation for the cycle's tragic irony.

Chapter 23: Literary Reflections – A New Age of Satire

In the gilded tapestry of human history, few periods have embraced the sheen of superficiality quite like the current era, where even our most profound crises are filtered through the cold comfort of touchscreens and algorithmic empathy. The writers of today, with their keen eyes and sharper keyboards, have taken up the quill—or rather, the stylus—to craft a new wave of satire that peels back the golden veneer, exposing the rusted innards of a society that dares to gloss over truth with a digital filter.

At first glance, the extravagance of wealth and innovation might suggest a tale of triumph. Neon metropolises stretch into skies painted artificial blue by a polluted haze, while the masses shuffle along, captured only as blurry figures in viral snapshots. Yet beneath this digital gloss lies a world ripe for the ironist's pen—one eager to illuminate the incongruities and absurdities of an age where opulence is accessible in pixels and prosperity remains elusive in practice.

Today's satirical writers operate in a realm where wit battles for attention amidst the cacophony of clickbait and misinformation. Their narratives are woven not only through ink and paper but through the ceaseless scroll of social media feeds. The craft of satire, once confined to pamphlets and theater, now gallops across a limitless digital landscape, igniting conversations one meme, one viral post at a time.

In this landscape, the novel has once again emerged as a piercing tool of cultural critique. Writers deftly dance across genres, spinning tales where the absurdity of a tech-saturated life looms large. Consider the dystopian delights scribbled by novelists who imagine worlds where social credits dictate human worth, and AI constructs govern love lives with all the warmth of a data breach. These literary architects not only mirror the world but prognosticate it—fusing humor with grim truth to reveal the sinuous connections between today's digital indulgences and tomorrow's realities.

Graphic novels and comic strips, too, have risen as sharp-edged mirrors to cultural excesses. The vibrant panels and terse dialogues, often dismissed in the past as juvenile, have morphed into potent tools of satire. Tackling subjects from meteorological mayhem to the microcosms of office culture, these visual narratives slice through the pretensions of modernity with both precision and punchlines, revealing a society simultaneously addicted to and at odds with its own self-created illusions.

Furthermore, podcasts and digital audio series have given voice to a new breed of satirists—those who couple the intimacy of the spoken word with the soaring reach of global networks. In the tradition of radio's golden age, these acerbic storytellers traverse topics ranging from political farce to pop culture grotesqueries, embedding critiques within sonic vignettes adorned with laughter as their backdrop. By dissecting today's ethical entanglements and laughable inconsistencies, these audio satirists transform the mundane treadmill of daily commutes into journeys replete with introspection and laughter.

It is essential to acknowledge, however, the paradox of this new age of satire: in a world increasingly characterized by dissonance and fragmentation, the purveyors of irony often find themselves both prophets and performers. Their sharp lenses demand engagement and introspection while simultaneously providing the escapism so desperately sought in turbulent times. In doing so, today's satirical voices offer a curious solace—one that assures us we are not alone in our bewilderment at the world's gilded absurdities.

In conclusion, as we traverse this gilded age updated and reinterpreted for a digital world, we rely on these literary satirists to guide us through the smoky haze of artificial glory and natural folly. From their words—dipped in irony and sharpened by prescient observation—we gather the courage to confront our world, one fraught with omens yet radiant with opportunities. Thus, perhaps, the greatest irony of all lies in the realization that the pixels assembling our lives into cohesive narratives may indeed illuminate the path to understanding, even as they playfully obscure it.

Chapter 24: Intermission Interrupted – The Case for Reformation

Pause, dear readers, and contemplate, if you will, the curious dance of time: the gilded stage of America, seemingly struck by a peculiar déjà vu, as society pauses at the intermission of progress only to find itself thrust back into the performance of "Change." The turn of the 20th century reverberates with the echoes of reform that as if with a mocking wink from history, resounds again in 2025.

As we cast our eyes to this contemporary tableau, one cannot help but marvel at the audacious echoes of the Progressive Era that now whisper with increasing vigor in today's political climate. In 1900, America stood at the precipice of reform, wrestling against the opulent chains of industrial excess and unchecked capitalism. Whether by unintended satire or an artful twist of fate, the corridors of 2025 have once again become the sounding board for calls of regulation and reform, as if flipping through a historied script with lines all too familiar.

Consider, if you will, the societal plight back in the days of muckrakers and magnates. Is the stage so different now when dissent festers beneath the polished façade of prosperity? The carriers of change now traverse digital highways rather than dusty roads, but they carry the same message: the masses crave balance amidst inequality, whispers of regulation hum sotto voce beneath the arias of partisan politics.

Yet, irony dances mischievously as these echoes infiltrate our contemporary epoch. Once, King Money roamed freely, lauded and lavishly untethered, crafting empires in iron and oil. Now, it's his digital progeny, the Technocrats, whose velvet grip around society's purse strings elicits calls for vigilant reimagination. Tech monopolies, like the trust giants before them, cast long, shimmering shadows where the light of reform seeks now to shine.

It begs the question, as we indulge the dialogue of our socioeconomic play: is history merely a revolving stage, a cycle infinitely looping between wealth and want? Or are we witnessing the satirical evolution of an age-old poster reaffirming that today's avant-garde reformers are merely tomorrow's institutionalists?

As much as technology pioneers or corporate titans may desire to play the role of the benevolent architects of our future, their modern-day power evokes the robber barons of old, necessitating regulatory counterweights every bit as robust as those employed a century ago. The regulatory whispers of 2025 merely repurpose an old refrain – that thriving humanity must be mirrored by a thriving humanity, not overshadowed by the machine-created avatars of progress.

In the spirit of irony, let us not forget the cacophony of voices clamoring for reform echo not solely from youth and idealism but also from the bastions of tradition and conservatism, now ironically lamenting empathetic oblivion. As shrewd observers from a past age – or indeed any age – might chuckle knowingly, perhaps it is this very clamor, this timeless desire for balance that, intended or not, serves as the perennial heartbeat of society.

Thus, as we press onward, it behooves us to ask: are we witnessing innovation taking flight, carrying the weight of inherited dreams? Or do we merely bear witness to yet another masquerade of reformation, an enduring theatre where actors change but the roles – and the ironies – remain timelessly the same? As the act of change resurfaces with familiar ardor, it is our erudite duty to observe, critique, and, perhaps, to not merely live through history, but thoughtfully rewrite it.

In closing this intermission of thought, may we step into the next act with a keener eye and a wiser heart, resolute in this knowledge: the call for reformation is not merely echoed, but critically essential, a narrative not only revisited but requited. After all, the intermission is only ever an interlude, not an end, as history instructs us with such elegant, ironic precision.

Chapter 25: The Invisible Line – Bridging Past and Present

When examining the enterprise of human civilization, we find that history holds an uncanny way of replaying the same script, but with different actors and slightly updated costumes. It has become something of an archetype—the Gilded Age saga of grotesque wealth and eye-watering opulence, juxtaposed with the squalor of its forgotten underbelly. In our saunter through the 21st century, a standing ovation should be afforded to our collective capacity to replicate this narrative. After all, why build bridges when you can dig trenches of inequality wider and deeper?

This chapter holds no pretense of imparting a groundbreaking revelation. On the contrary, it is an ode to our remarkable consistency, a toast to our unfailing memory when it comes to perpetuating iniquities rather than learning from them. It is a commendable feat of societal dedication that warrants closer examination.

Let us rewind to the dawn of the original Gilded Age, a time defined by titans of industry, unbridled capitalism, and philanthropic gestures tempered with self-serving motives. In the late 19th century, names like Vanderbilt, Carnegie, and Rockefeller prefixed the pantheon of American lore, casting long shadows over both Wall Street and the tenements huddled under its gaze. Their empires rose as monuments to ambition and innovation, pillars of an economy surging towards the future with chest-thumping bravado. Yet, beneath their gilded facades lay steel skeletons built with the sweat and toil of uncelebrated multitudes—immigrants clinging to the ladder's lower rungs in hope of a better tomorrow, which for many, remained unwritten history.

Fast-forward to 2025, and we find ourselves gathered under a strikingly similar marquee, preparing for a familiar performance. The principal actors may have changed, and the corporate logos may bear contemporary fonts, but the act remains stubbornly monochrome. Our modern titans, draped in tech-fuelled wealth, have mastered not only the art of resource hoarding but also the subtle craft of tax avoidance. A new lexicon of wealth amusement graces our ears, filled with acronyms assembled from bits and bytes. Yet, for all their innovative gloss, these new emperors tread old paths, leaving the same footprints of disparity in their wake.

Now, enter stage: income inequality—our reliably persistent character in the grand historical production. While the "roaring" successes of our era lounge in penthouse suites and enclosed worlds of luxury, those responsible for constructing those ivory towers are often omitted from the guest list. The modern workforce, adaptive and resilient, crowds the gig economy's labyrinth, a precarious maze overflowing with mismatched benefits and uncertain sustenance.

Ah! The sweet symphony of progress accompanies the joyful chorus of economic disparity, echoing through our cities, both old and new. Our ancestors of the Gilded Age would nod approvingly at our dedication; the disparity sloughs on with vigorous enthusiasm.

Moreover, it seems we have honed our prowess at providing palliative solutions to the wounds of inequality while skirting any meaningful surgery. The charitable gestures and philanthropic rhetoric decorate our newsfeeds and press releases, shrouded nobly in corporate social responsibility statements. Beneath the veneer of charitable tax deductions lies a quieter truth: a keen affinity for business as usual.

And yet, do not brand this ironic reflection as one of pure cynicism. For where is there an irony without the hope of change, the tickle of possibility that tomorrow may rewrite the script? It loiters here, interlaced within these cynical stitches, daring us to reimagine the invisible line, to wield our mighty digital tools for connection rather than division.

So, as we step off this temporal bridge and stare into the pages yet to be penned, let us hold dear this specific: the power of transformation lies clenched in the collective hands of both hereditary magnates and their societal nomads. A union in purpose may yet usher forth a prelude more harmonious than any glitzy age that has come before. Until then, we find solace in the pockets of progress and stir the pot of possibility, lest we fall encore to yesteryear's gilded temptations.

Chapter 26: A Gilded Future – What Lies Beyond 2025?

As we stand at the threshold of 2025, it is difficult not to look back at the kaleidoscopic spectacle of America's Gilded Age without a chuckle of irony. After all, history, with its insatiable penchant for irony, seems to delight in repeating itself. Just as America in the late 19th century brimmed with opulence, inequality, and rapid technological advancements, so too does our present era echo with familiar refrains. Yet, standing on this precarious precipice, we are offered an opportunity—not merely to see the repeating patterns but to reimagine a narrative that steps beyond mere mimicry of past foibles.

More than a century ago, the Gilded Age was a term coined by Mark Twain and Charles Dudley Warner, alluding to the glistening veneer that masked societal ills. Today, we find ourselves under the shimmering blanket of our own gilded epoch, where technological marvels coexist uneasily beside glaring inequities. The lessons of Grover Cleveland's time—of vast wealth accumulations in hands that could never quite touch the working class—whisper to us from the grave of history, only to be sometimes drowned out by the lure of shiny new gadgets and promises of digital utopias.

But could it be that humanity, possessed as it is with the chronic illness of selective historical amnesia, continues on this path not because it must, but because it is seduced by the inevitable irony of it all? It is a question worthy of deep reflection. For if irony is our unseen albatross, then America's grand narrative is one that seems to revel in its persistent embrace.

Yet, within this ironic repetition, hope persists—a curious flame that burns despite the odds, fueled by the possibility that this time, things could indeed be different. Perhaps our forebears have left us more than just technological marvels and architectural grandeur; they have left footprints in the sands of time that warn and instruct as much as inspire. In those footprints lies a map directing us toward meaningful reform, genuine equity, and human-centric progress.

To imagine what lies beyond 2025 is to envision a future where we do not die the deaths of our ancestors—those choked by the gilded façades and smokestacks of their time—but live new lives born out of informed introspection and concerted action. We stand equipped with the hindsight they lacked, armed with the potential of technology they couldn't fathom. The key, then, is whether we choose to use these gifts to gild our future with genuine progress rather than superficial brilliance.

So, what lies beyond 2025? The answer, dripping with irony as it may be, seems to rest in the very lessons history has laid bare for us: that the grandeur of any age is measured not by its wealth but by its humanity. That the gilding worth pursuing is the one that uplifts rather than drowns, that enlightens rather than exploits. In embracing this ethos, the splendor of the now need not eclipse the hope for a gilded future, grounded in egalitarian values and imbued with authentic prosperity.

If only irony weren't such a compelling character in the grand American saga, one could almost believe that history's lessons might finally be learned. And yet, the hopeful endnote that resonates as 2025 unfolds is this—should we elect to, despite the relentless lure of irony, we may yet script a future as luminous as the gilded dreams that tantalize us. Only this time, let it be one built upon a foundation of fairness, inclusion, and sustainable progress. A gilded future indeed—should we dare to grasp it.

Epilogue

As we close the chapter on "The Gilded Age Revisited: An Ironic Reflection from Opulence to 2025," we are compelled to confront the cyclical nature of history—a history that, perhaps ironically, seems determined to teach us lessons we are equally determined to ignore. As we gaze back to the Gilded Age of the late 19th century with its glittering facade obscuring deep social chasms, and then forward to our own era with its neon glow of technological advancement shadowing a similar narrative of disparity, the parallels are as clear as they are ironic.

Then, as now, burgeoning economic wealth concentrated in the hands of a few painted a veneer of prosperity over the realities of social inequity and political corruption. The titans of industry of yesteryears—those magnates wielding unchecked influence—have found their echoes in today's tech barons and financial oligarchs. Their empires, built on the ideal of innovation, mirror the grandeur and audacity of skyscrapers piercing into the skyline, yet casting long shadows over the labor force sustaining their base. The opulence of the past is paralleled by the digital opulence of the present—luxuries so advanced they border on alchemical magic, all the while leaving the existential plights of many unaddressed.

The irony lies not merely in the repetition of history, but in the modern complicity to it—an era punctuated by climate crises, stark socio-economic divides, and a global political stage swaying under the weight of hyper-partisan agendas. The vanities of the Gilded Age—champagne bubbles of fleeting delight at extravagant galas—find their contemporary parallel in social media's ephemeral moments of triumph, in echo chambers rather than ballrooms. We are entertained, just as the industrialists ensured their legacies through art and endowments, with a veneer of progress serving to distract from underlying discrepancies.

Yet, in recasting this familiar play, we must ask ourselves, are we destined to be captive actors in a drama we did not script? Must we again feign surprise when the glitz proves hollow? History offers neither comfort nor cruelty, only lessons in human nature. It is within our grasp to seize the wisdom of hindsight, daring to chart a course untangling us from these gilded cycles. Embrace the irony, the historians invite, not as an endearing quirks of fate but as a catalyst for change.

To progress purposefully, we must employ a clearer vision—one that questions unchecked power, that prioritizes community and environmental stewardship over unsustainable expansion. Let us engage in discourse not for dissent's sake but for solutions that blend economic vitality with social responsibility. We must look beyond the commercial dazzle to ensure that our advancing technologies serve as bridges rather than barriers. In the irony lies an opportunity—how deliciously poetic that where the past misstepped, the present might correct its gait.

Therefore, as the ink dries on this volume, we challenge you, dear reader, to step beyond spectatorship into participatory advocacy. Let history's irony fuel a future where opulence is redefined as the rich tapestry of united human effort shared equitably, and true progress is marked by the upliftment of every voice. Cast off the gilded chains of old; with the wisdom of hindsight as our compass, let us, for perhaps the first time, gild the future not in gold but in genuine, shared human prosperity.

Appendix

Timeline

-1869-1877: "Ulysses S. Grant Administration – The Age of Scandal"

- 1869: The Transcontinental Railroad is completed, ushering an era where manifest destiny meets corporate monopoly; economy inevitably follows.

- 1870: Standard Oil is founded by John D. Rockefeller, an effort to standardize wealth distribution — predominantly in his favor.

- 1872: Credit Mobilier Scandal, a blueprint for future corporate-government synergy.

- 1873: The Panic of 1873 — because nothing says "Gilded Age" like financial instability and widespread unemployment wrapped in a shiny industrial veneer.

1877-1900: "Mark Twain's Guide to Irony and American Progress"

- 1877: Rutherford B. Hayes assumes presidency through an amicable exchange of electoral votes, gracefully bypassing popular mandates.

- 1890: The Sherman Antitrust Act passes — a legislative attempt to make monopolistic titans shake (with laughter).

- 1893: The Chicago World's Fair showcases technological marvels amidst economic despair, proving nothing captivates the masses like a good paradox.

- 1896: The election of William McKinley reaffirms the public's endearing trust in corporate-sponsored governance.

1900-2025: "Echoes of Gilded Glimmer"

- 1929: The Great Depression begins, illustrating a timeless lesson in the cyclical nature of economic boom and bust.

- 1980-2000: The rise of the Reagan Era exemplifies the enduring charm of supply-side economics, much like a Gilded Age sequel.

- 2008: The Great Recession rekindles reliance on financial institutions' self-regulation, because history evidently only repeats the finest acts.

- 2020: Covid-19 pandemic exposes economic disparities with startling clarity, as if inequality needed a spotlight.

- 2025: Corporations continue to influence politics, proving the resilience of 19th-century legacies.

Additional Reading Resources

- "The Robber Barons" by Matthew Josephson: An insightful dive into the titans of industry, perfect for anyone curious about how few hands can shape a nation's wealth.

- "Capital in the Twenty-First Century" by Thomas Piketty: Offers a rich analysis of economic inequalities beautifully resonating with the Gilded Age ethos.

- "The Theory of the Leisure Class" by Thorstein Veblen: Explore the origins of "conspicuous consumption" and understand why flaunting wealth never goes out of style.

- "Plutocrats: The Rise of the New Global Super-Rich and the Fall of Everyone Else" by Chrystia Freeland: A contemporary account of wealth patterns, proving the Gilded Age plays on repeat.

Key Acts and Statutes

- The Interstate Commerce Act (1887): Signed to regulate the railroads, showcasing faith in regulation to tame corporate giants while loopholes drag their feet.

- The Homestead Act (1862): Fuelled westward expansion, laying foundations for land speculation — a novelty in equitable growth.

- The Sherman Antitrust Act (1890): A well-intentioned legislative tool, wielded as effectively against labor unions as against monopolies.

- The Dodd-Frank Wall Street Reform and Consumer Protection Act (2010): An attempt to tame modern financial systems in a nod to earlier eras' attempts at regulatory oversight.

- Citizens United v. FEC (2010): Legal confirmation that wealth speaks louder, preserving the Gilded Age's spirit of financial influence in politics.

This appendix concludes with a nod to the cycle of hyper-capitalism and inequality that is perennially revisited. Just as in "The Gilded Age," today's enthralling dance between opulence and irony continues, unabated and entirely predictable. Ah, progress — doesn't it precisely echo the graceful arc of a boomerang?

Endnote

As we cast our retrospective gaze from the tentative brink of 2025, it is difficult not to marvel at the peculiar spectacles of history—particularly the flamboyant display known as the Gilded Age. This era, a richly ornamented chapter of American excess in the late 19th century, serves as both a mirror and a mirage, reflecting truths and tempting us with illusions. One might be forgiven for seeing the irony in our contemporary fascination with its lavishness, as our own age, teetering precariously on the edge of technological wonders and socio-economic disparities, often echoes its laughable contradictions and relentless aspirations.

The Gilded Age was, let us remember, a period wrapped in irony even at its inception. Coined by Mark Twain and Charles Dudley Warner, the term captures the era's veneer of gold—a deceptive gloss on the surface of systemic corruption, unchecked capitalism, and vast social inequities. It was an age when titans of industry, with names that resonate through history like a roll call of avarice—Carnegie, Rockefeller, and Vanderbilt—constructed their empires with little regard for those who toiled in the shadows of their prosperity. These men were the patron saints of material accumulation, their legacies etched in libraries and foundations, seemingly in an effort to varnish their ruthless pursuits with a thin patina of benevolence.

Yet here we are in 2025, our own world festooned with a digital gilding of its own making. As we sift through the sagas of Silicon Valley's wunderkinder or marvel at the dizzying altitudes of billionaire-fueled space odysseys, how can we not draw parallels to the barons of the past? Contemporary titans, with fortunes made not in steel or oil but in data and innovation, invite us to ponder whether humanity has truly advanced or simply swapped its tools of majesty. One could argue that we are witnessing a new form of opulence, now digitized and existing in virtual realms—where influence is measured in followers and likes, rather than lands and tenements.

But to engage solely in drawing stark parallels between then and now would be to miss the more nuanced ironies threaded through both eras. Consider the social movements and labor reforms born of the Gilded Age's industrial discontent. These efforts, wrought in struggle and sacrifice, claim credit for laying the groundwork for our own world of rights and reform. Yet, we find ourselves still entangled in debates over income inequality, corporate ethics, and the evolving definitions of work. It's as if the ghosts of Pullman strikes and Haymarket affairs linger in boardrooms and on battlegrounds of modern political discourse.

The Gilded Age, in its sprawling tapestry of contradiction, serves as a quintessential lesson on the cyclical nature of human ambition. It is a testament to our perpetual dance between progress and pitfalls, between visions of utopia and the harsher truths of reality. The era's outward splendor and inner turmoil remind us, albeit ironically, that history is seldom a linear ascent. Instead, it is a series of loops and eddies, a narrative that, much like our current trajectory, is destined to unfurl with complexities and surprises.

As we conclude this exploration of opulence through the ages, one is drawn to reflect, with a wry smile, on the enduring human penchant for excess. The Gilded Age was but a chapter, albeit a gaudily illustrated one, in the grand tome of time. And so, as we stand at the doorstep of this new gilded epoch—our age of algorithmic alchemy and digitized dreams—we might do well to remember the lessons gilded in the laughter, folly, and fortitude of those who came before. History may not repeat itself exactly, but, as the saying goes, it certainly rhymes, often with an irony audible to those willing to listen.

Made in the USA
Columbia, SC
07 December 2024